I0541739

Formed In Experiences

Formed In Experiences

BLAKE TODD

Text Blake Todd

Design StoryTerrace

Copyright © Blake Todd

Text is private and confidential

First print January 2023

CONTENTS

DEDICATION

I was encouraged by so many to share these stories as people wanted to know more. Constantly I was asked why bitterness, hate, and vengeance was not part of the story. How is it that these experiences fueled the desire to understand and forgive rather than sue or seek revenge. The two people most responsible for helping to form my inner desire to empathize, question and embrace all sides of a story - the whole story, are my parents – Roger and Mary. With all my heart and love, this book is dedicated to you.

No book in any form ever makes it to print without help. Either a muse to help motivate, a transcriber to take the oral story and bring it to print, or an editor to fine tune and massage it into shape. The list is long, but I wanted to especially thank Michael who got this over the finish line – Now that we have found each other, I look forward to bigger projects together.

1

BULLETS IN BEIRUT

April 17th, 1975.

It was my last night in Beirut, and I was going to make the most of it. Especially after the three days of hell we'd just gone through.

Of course, I never realized when the sun awoke me on that day in 1975 that my last night in Beirut would come awfully close to being my last night on earth.

I was in Beirut in April 1975 on a two-week term break from Pepperdine University's Year-in-Europe program, in Heidelberg, where I had spent two of my three sophomore semesters. Beirut was my term-break destination because it had been "home" to me, ever since my parents, Roger and Mary, had moved to the city from California two years earlier when my father was promoted to head up Lockheed International's Middle East operation.

An idea that resonated with me with each visit to Beirut was that home is not a place or a building; it is wherever the people that you love are. One of my "people" was my dog, Sheko, who had joined our family after our return from Hong Kong. Dogs were not allowed in college dorms and certainly not in cramped quarters in a European study abroad program, so he was now with my mother in Beirut. And while I would see my mother and my dog, I wasn't going to see my father on this trip, as he was traveling on business and was due back the day I was leaving. On many occasions throughout my life, he had been traveling, and we accepted this for who he was and what he did. Even so, I was sorry that I was going to be leaving on the day of my father's 46th birthday. Maybe we'd celebrate it together next year.

Even though I had been to Beirut a few times before, tonight was different. No one was shooting in the streets; the sub-machine gun nest on our apartment building roof was gone; and I was making dinner for Karen, a blond beauty whom I'd met about 10 days earlier through my mother's networking with the other expat ladies in town.

My mother wanted me to have friends when I was in Beirut on this trip because the last time I was here, I had no friends my own age and got bored, winding up in Bahrain and then in the hospital. That could be a complete book unto itself, but we will get to that story later.

My mother and Lynne Fetterholf conspired to arrange a meeting of their two kids—not quite a blind date, but in the zone. Lynne and her husband, Andy, a Middle East Airlines pilot, like all the American expats in Beirut in the 1970s, knew my parents from crossing paths at the Royal Lebanon

Golf Club, volunteering at the American Women's charity craft shop, dining at the elegant Phoenician Hotel, or having a cocktail at the beach club.

Karen was visiting her parents in Beirut before attending the University of Maryland in the fall, and my mother saw a golden opportunity for her only son to have some company while in town. Karen and I were the same age, and we were in the same city, so it seemed only natural we should spend some time together.

When I first saw Karen, I could not believe my luck—and my mother's excellent judgment. She was a model, in demand for fashion shoots, and it was easy to see why: With her blond hair, her clean, almost Scandinavian facial lines, and her figure that was womanly without being too curvy, the camera loved her. She was a rarity in that part of the world and sought after for being a lovely, blond, blue-eyed young American.

As for me, well, I was not a model. Closing in on six feet but only getting there if I wore cowboy boots, I was described as being more skin and bones than any sort of slender male model, weighing maybe 105 pounds. When I was younger, my mother said I should be a model for Care Packages, I was so thin.

Oh, and I was looking out at the world, and at Karen, through glasses whose new plastic lenses were not exactly the thickness of Coke bottles. But they were close.

I had never dated a girl as attractive as Karen before—

if dating was what we were doing. Maybe she saw spending time with me as a favor to her mother. Maybe she saw me as a sorry specimen who would improve by basking in her radiance. Maybe I was just another guy she had to tolerate for 10 days. I stopped worrying about the "maybes" and just decided to enjoy my good fortune, and Karen, and having someone my own age to hang with for the almost two-week break.

My parents' car, a manual Austin American, was mine to use when I liked, which was a bonus because I knew my way around the city and could impress Karen with my Lebanese driving skills. I even knew the shortcuts to get to her parents' apartment on the opposite side of town rather quickly, driving down through the street that bisected the Palestinian camp near where we lived and then taking some of the less-traveled side streets to avoid the Beirut traffic, which had one law: There was no law.

The city was still foreign to me in its ways and means, but I had its streets pretty well figured out. Once Karen and I were together, there was no urgency to get anywhere fast. I was just happy to be in her company because she seemed to like mine, and so much of that is half the battle. As for those shortcuts, I didn't always take them because my desire to spend more time with Karen might have aimed my internal GPS at the long and more scenic route to get from A to B.

Karen lived in the Hamra district, and I would pick her up and then would point the Austin toward the Phoenician Hotel and get on the Corniche that hugged the ocean all the way around the city. The real name of the road was the Avenue Général de Gaulle or Paris Road, but everyone referred to it as the Corniche. It is a beautiful drive along the rough and rocky coastline of the Mediterranean, whose sea waves glistened and sprayed as the sun shone and warmed us.

Beirut Hamara street scene 1975

Across the Corniche from the Phoenician Hotel there was another hotel located right on the shore of the Mediterranean Sea, the St. Georges, where we could rent speedboats and water ski. The Mediterranean waters were choppy, and it wasn't the best idea to ski beyond the boat's wake, but many did it just to say they had. I was not one of them. But as in California, Beirut offered the adventurous a chance to ski in the mountains and then to water ski on the Mediterranean on the same day.

Beirut Coastline along the Corniche 1975

Karen and I had a great week together. We shopped in the souks in central Beirut. "Souk" is a variation on the Arabic *sūq*, which means "market," and that's exactly what the souk is in North Africa and the Middle East. It's a marketplace where you can pretty much find whatever you need or even don't need (except anything illegal). In Beirut, these outdoor stalls selling food shared space with shops that had been there for centuries. Shops still run by the families who had started them hundreds of years ago.

The pungent odors of the spices, the light streaming between the overhanging canopies of the tightly packed-in stalls, and the sounds of Arabic, with a bit of French and English crackling in the air, created a sensory experience unlike anything I had known. The vendors in these stalls had their spaces passed down through the generations. In many cases, the wares were the same as those sold centuries ago. If you sold pottery in the 12th century, you may still be selling pottery in the 20th.

Beirut Golk souk 1974

Karen had an easy laugh, and it delighted me that I could summon it from her as we shopped at the "donkey bead" store or while we window-shopped at the storefronts in the gold souk. We sat on the warm sand at the beach club, and we took paddleboards out toward the Mediterranean rocks with the lapping waves breaking around us. As time passed, my initial heart-thumping attraction to Karen had become a friendship. Which is not to say I did not want to take our friendship to the next level, to lean in and kiss Karen and have her kiss me back. I had four days left in my Beirut spring break to see if that wish would come true.

And then the shooting started and blew my dreams of romance with Karen into smithereens. Or so I thought.

To understand why the shooting started, one needs to understand the rainbow that was Lebanon and how the colors of that rainbow shifted until the country was drenched in blood. There is a saying about Lebanon—true then and now—that "No two fingers are identical, but it's all the same hand." This meant that the hand of Lebanon had an unwritten agreement that assigned the three highest government positions—the three biggest fingers—to people of the country's three dominant religions. The president was to be a Maronite Christian, the parliamentary speaker a Shiite Muslim, and the premier a Sunni Muslim.

This political arrangement was designed to keep the peace, but it also became a source of bitterness, and then bloodshed. When it was created in 1943, when Lebanon was granted its independence from what was then Free France during World War II, there was a certain cold-eyed pragmatism to it. It was based on the relative populations of each of these three power-sharing groups, which were similar in size when Lebanon achieved independence.

However, there were 17 other religious minorities in the country, and the economy had an alarming gap between its wealthiest, who were predominantly Christians and Sunni Muslims, and those in refugee camps, who lived in abject poverty. Those were the other two fingers on the hand. And they wanted their fair share of the riches.

The religious composition of Lebanon had changed since the end of World War II so that by 1975, Muslims made up 75% of the country's population. Lebanon had accepted many seeking asylum—Armenians, Kurds, and Palestinians, all of whom changed the political dynamics constantly and all of whom had national aspirations in other places, which boiled over in Lebanon.

So, too, did Israel's "scorched earth" policy in southern Lebanon in the early 1970s, which forced Shiite Muslim peasants to the north. The Shiites didn't like the Sunnis and vice versa, and these family conflicts were straining relations within the Muslim community. As a result, the minority Christian groups, known as the Phalangists, got nervous. And so they trained and maintained militias to protect their positions.

The Palestinian refugee camp, Mar Elias, was just down the street from my parents' apartment. The hodgepodge of buildings, huts, and dilapidated dwellings that were stacked up upon one another was in the south of the city, near the last major roundabout as you left Beirut to travel south, near where the Spinneys Center grocery store was at the time. It was under the flight path for the Beirut international airport, and while we tend to think of Beirut as a crowded, cheek-by-jowl city, the area in which we lived had not yet been developed completely. Our apartment building was the only one on that block that could have easily fit half a dozen big apartment buildings.

View of Mar Elis from our apartment - February 1974

But our neighbor, and a close one, was the Mar Elias refugee camp—one of the largest and oldest Palestinian refugee camps in existence. Mar Elias was founded in 1952 by the Congregation of St. Elias to host Palestine refugees from the Galilee region of Palestine. It was inhabited mainly by Christian Palestinians, as well as a large non-Palestinian population. It was two city blocks long by one block wide and bisected in the middle by Dr. Philippe Hitti Street.

Our apartment building was a half a block to the south on the other side of Gabriel El Murr Boulevard. The entire camp had walls, at least 12 feet high, surrounding it, with the entrances to each of the two halves of the camp in the center of its bisecting street. Buildings were wedged in tightly beside each other with multiple stories and shaky staircases, letting limited light down onto the pathways. In places, they were barely wide enough for a motorbike to pass through. I knew that I could look at it, but I could not enter it. It was so close and yet so forbidden. And soon, it would come crashing down on me.

On April 13th, 1975, a bus carrying Palestinians was attacked by Phalangists in the Christian suburb of Ein Rummaneh. The attack was in revenge for a Palestinian attack on a Christian baptism a few days earlier, in which the baptized child's father was killed.

In the revenge attack, 27 Palestinians were killed. Fighting then erupted in those areas of Beirut that were controlled by those two groups. It had not yet taken over the entire city, but even so, Beirut shut down because of the outburst of violence, and everyone sheltered in place.

Barbed wire and a divided city - April 1975

During this battle, most of the fighting was in other areas of the city. Even so, the Palestinians from the Mar Elias refugee camp, which we could see from our building, realized that this sight line of ours could be useful to them in protecting their camp. They set up a lookout position on top of our apartment building, complete with a sub-machine gun team looking for threats—or people and things—to shoot at. This made our apartment building a potential target should the violence sweep our way. I could imagine one sectarian group or another seeing the Palestinians on the roof and then opening fire at our building.

The fighting lasted for three days, and for three days, we didn't leave our apartment building. Gunfire popped during the day and then increased in volume and frequency during the night. Explosions happened often enough to convince, Sheko, my dog, to be happy with his walks inside the apartment building's courtyard. He didn't mind at all, as he wasn't fond of Arab men, and they were not fond of him. And as they could now convey their displeasure with bullets, he, like us, was safest out of their sight. Even our apartment building had its own walls surrounding it.

Still, our apartment wasn't completely safe, either. We kept our movements to the interior hallway as much as possible because it was hidden from the windows that were in every room. We didn't want to be in front of a window because we knew snipers were on top of our building, so they were probably everywhere else, too.

The airport had been closed, so not only was my father not able to get back to Beirut from his business trip, but I had also resigned myself to the fact that I would most likely be late getting back to Heidelberg. There was no 24-7 CNN yet, and the cableverse did not exist, so what news we got of the war outside our building came from scattered BBC reports on TV and radio. And the amazing grapevine of information shared by the maids in the building. How or where they got the information was always a mystery. All we cobbled together from the news reports and the maids was that the Beirut powers were trying to broker a truce.

So, we decided to make the best of it. We had to eat, so everyone in the apartment building thought we might as well eat together. My mother and I and our neighbors created progressive dinners that would start in one apartment for one course and then we would move through the building to sample the next course from different apartments. We could use the interior stairwell to move from floor to floor with what we thought was safety, but if the guys on the roof had been twitchy and come down the stairs, that notion would have been blasted to bits.

And to keep the peace, we even shared tea in the elevator lobbies on our floors with the Palestinians who were manning the lookout on top of our building. These men were polite, and we had seen them in the neighborhood for a long time. They knew us, and we knew them. We were not afraid of them. We were afraid of what was outside.

During the day, there wasn't much to do sitting in that hallway. I read books and played gin rummy with my mother, and I learned to do needlepoint. I even finished one small canvas of the hand of Fatima. Sheko, the dog, was brushed constantly, as it was better than having his nervous shedding swirl around the confined space. And I felt bad for the guy, as he was nervous at the sounds of gunfire that could be heard all through the day and night.

Fortunately, the phones still worked, and I was able to talk with Karen. We were both getting sad that the violence had cut short my time in Beirut, and we lamented the fact that I was leaving on the 18th—if the airport reopened. We promised to write and stay in touch, but in the back of my mind, I knew that this was a vacation friendship. We wouldn't have anything that would bind us to keep it going across the physical distance between us. Still, in the expat community, friendships are made quicker and deeper than in just about any other community, and so I really didn't know what would become of us. But, one can dream, can't they?

And then, to our surprise and delight, a ceasefire was called on the 16th of April. And I had a plan to celebrate my last night in Beirut in style. I called Karen and invited her to dinner—at my parents' apartment. I would cook dinner, as many of the restaurants had not yet reopened.

I was a good cook, but I wasn't fast. So it took me the better part of the day to whip up, slowly, the feast of new potatoes, peeled steamed asparagus, and sauteed veal for my mom; her seven-months-pregnant friend, Lotus; Karen; and myself. Then, after dinner, Lotus and my mother went to Lotus's apartment, and Karen and I had some time together.

And I finally got to kiss her, and she kissed me back. We knew that my mother and Lotus could come back at any minute, so we kept it mild, and we talked a lot and then kissed a bit more. As much as my young hormones may have wanted things to heat up, the cool warning of my mother's imminent return tamped them down. Along with my inexperience and the fear that I would not know what to do or what the tells were for taking additional steps.

Then as midnight came around, just like in a fairytale, it was time for the ball to end and the princess to depart. Besides, we had agreed that I would take Karen home so her parents would not worry. So with our small four-door Austin America serving as the chariot and midnight fast approaching, I would drive the fastest route to her apartment. It was a route that I knew so well, one that started straight on our street and went down Dr. Philippe Hitti Street through the Palestinian camp.

It was very dark as we drove between the high walls of the Palestinian camp. Only the car's headlights illuminated the road ahead. As I approached the halfway point of that block and the gates into the camp were coming up, Palestinian guards came out of nowhere and waved at me to stop. The problem was that I had driven past them before I saw them in the rearview mirror. Then time started going in ultra-slow motion so that I could remember the next 10 seconds for as long as I lived . . .

We were now about 50 yards past the waving guards, and I looked into the rearview mirror and saw three men step out from the darkened recesses of the camp entrances. All three had Kalashnikov rifles and started firing their weapons at the car. I did not see too much of the firing, though, as the rearview mirror was shot away, rattling around and coming to rest in my lap. The windshield was blown away, and it seemed like a million shattered pieces were flying everywhere. I glanced to my right to check on Karen, and that glance caused my head to move slightly to the left as two bullets took away some of the headrest and glanced off my forehead instead of through the back of my skull. And my vision suddenly became tinged with red.

I looked over at Karen, who was breathing heavily but seemed to be unhurt.

Instinctively, I had depressed the accelerator to the floor, and the end of the street was upon us as I turned hard to the left at the corner, instinctively knowing I had to get out of the line of fire, which was visible now as tracer rounds were part of the mix, every third bullet lighting up as it aimed to kill Karen and me. The small Austin America car is not known for its handling ability, and it came close to rolling over, as the left turn I had made at top speed had the car on two wheels and nearly coming off the road. The sounds of Kalashnikov rifles firing at us were replaced with the sounds of tires straining to keep purchase with the road.

I took my foot off the floorboard, righting the car, but kept us moving at a rapid pace down the street. Now the world was not just tinged in red but had a red overlay on top of everything. My hand reached to my forehead, and I felt the warm current of blood coming from a hole in my head. I had been shot in the head! And I knew we had to go even faster until we reached safety; before the bullet that hit my head killed me. I heard Karen starting to breathe heavily, and with my adrenaline at full speed, I yelled at her, "You will be fine, but don't look at me!" I didn't want her to panic at the sight of my blood. And I knew that life at that moment became very simple, and my mission was very clear. Just keep us both alive.

2

AN INTERNATIONAL YOUTH

I was born in a palace. Well, not really, but the Naval Hospital in San Diego, California, is also known as the Pink Palace. It is named for the color of the Spanish Colonial Revival architecture that characterizes the administration building, built in 1920 in Balboa Park, which is also home to the San Diego Zoo. It is a fine place to be born, and so I was, very quickly, on August 20th, 1955.

My father, Roger, had just been promoted to Lieutenant, Junior Grade, in the United States Navy, so having a baby in the Navy hospital was, as my mother, Mary, liked to say, essentially free. She had already given birth to my sister, Joyce, almost three years earlier, and as the saying goes, the second baby can emerge faster than the time it took to create the baby. My mother was on the beach until the afternoon of the day I was born. Webb Colter, a close family friend and one of my father's fraternity brothers, was there with her when she said it was time to go to the hospital. Webb got her there, then called my dad, who barely made it to the hospital in time.

It was quick on the other end, too, as my mother was in and out of the hospital on the same day that she gave birth to me. She was just there long enough to accept the zinnia that my father had picked, which an orderly had presented to her in a glass jar, and to take her first good look at me when the nurses presented me for inspection. She decided that I looked enough like my father's father to be the right baby, and that was good enough for her.

My parents had met in high school and had gone to UCLA together. When my father joined the Navy, they were assigned to San Diego, and when I was born, we lived in a tiny one-bedroom apartment—you needed to walk through a closet to get to the bedroom. It's easy to think, given a lifetime of world travels, that I was born with the proverbial silver spoon in my mouth. I was born with the idea of a silver spoon somewhere on my being, and I have spent a lot of my life so far finding that spoon in unexpected places.

My father had joined the Navy because he wanted to go to sea, even though he got seasick. After I was born, my mother figured out why he never shipped out. She had dear family friends who looked out for her and her mother, and one of them, Ken Hull, had a friend in the Navy who agreed to keep Roger a landlubber so that their friend's daughter would not be made a widow with two small children.

When my dad left the Navy in 1956, he remained in the Navy reserves and got a job with Lockheed Aircraft Services in Ontario, California, which is 40 miles due east of Los Angeles. We were living on my father's salary, and when it looked like he was going to get posted to Vietnam with the reserves, he said goodbye to them. He wasn't going to leave my mother and his two kids alone now. Little did we know that my father would spend a lot of our lives away from us, but back then, we were very happy he wanted to stay put.

In 1960, that old family friend Ken Hull became president of Lockheed International, and my father joined his team. The Lockheed office where my father worked was in downtown Los Angeles, and so we moved to La Cañada, which was a bedroom community for downtown that had a school district considered to be first rate. La Cañada is 15 miles north of central LA, and if you ask me today what my hometown is, I say that it is La Cañada.

I had a very happy childhood on Oakwood Avenue, taking swimming lessons in the summer and enjoying life in our big backyard. My dad put in a pool in 1965, the last year we were there, and I loved being in the water. My father, on the other hand, used to joke that he swam in it so seldom because of travel that the cost per swim for him was pretty high. We had chickens in our backyard until a raccoon took them all right through the wire of the chicken coop. There were other kids my age on our street that I played with— Gary, Jimmy, and Tim were three—as the town was one of those places that attracted lots of young families. I enjoyed school and was a good student until I started to have health issues.

I experienced frequent sore throats and ear infections, and those problems got worse so that swallowing became painful. My mom used to worry a lot because of my health, partially because when I was about a year old, I got very sick and very dehydrated—to the point that the doctors said it may have stunted my growth. One day, we visited the family doctor, Dr. Melvin Purdy, in our neighborhood. He did some tests, which suggested to him that I had severe tonsilitis. But in reality, it only took the tongue depressor and a look into my throat to get to his diagnosis. It was a relief to my mother, as many kids develop inflamed tonsils and have a tonsillectomy—which removes the gland that becomes inflamed—to correct the problem. But it was also a new concern for her and my father, as it meant I would have to have an operation.

At the time, tonsils and adenoids were considered expendable, like your appendix is when it becomes inflamed. My doctor told my mother, "Like any surgical procedure, however, there are risks of complications such as bleeding and infection. It's also a painful procedure that can involve a week or more of moderate to severe pain."

My mother sensed that he wanted to say more. He did. He told her that if the operation failed, then I could develop other allergies and breathing issues, as the tonsils and adenoids are the first line of defense against viruses and other airborne allergens. He also felt it helpful to add that anesthesia was also a risk—as in I might not wake up from it.

My mother asked to use a phone so she could speak to my father. I sat still in the clinic chair, my throat sore, observing the fish swimming in the aquarium that acted as a room divider. When my mother came back, she silently signed the permission letter for my operation. And with her promises that I would get to eat ice cream and stay home from school to watch television, soothing any fears I might have had, the next morning, I was in the hospital and going under the knife.

The operation was not as successful as we had hoped. I was hospitalized for more than a week. When I was discharged, the swelling in my throat and face took longer to diminish than expected. For a terribly skinny boy to spend any time at all on a liquid diet only worried my mother further.

I was in good spirits, though. Even though I was in the first grade, I had a belief that things would work out for the best. Dr. Purdy had a great bedside manner and that quiet confidence that ensured trust as well. Plus, I accepted that what is, is, even at that young age. It remains one of my life philosophies today.

My belief that all would work out was only reinforced when, within a month, what had been an "unsuccessful" recovery was complete, and the outcome appeared to take care of all my aggravating symptoms. I could speak without hurting my throat. I could chew and eat food as well. For my last checkup, the doctor ordered an X-ray of my throat.

And he was in disbelief when he studied it. "I cannot believe this, Mary! This is incredible!" My throat was perfectly fine. My mother hugged me, and her face was wet. "Thank God!" she whispered, then planted a kiss on my forehead. "It's all because of your patient belief that it would be OK! I love you a lot!" she whispered again. I responded, "All that ice cream didn't hurt!"

Little did we know that I wasn't done with my health problem. By the time third grade rolled around at Oak Grove Elementary, other kids had begun to think I was "slow" and pushed me around. I wasn't ignoring them—I was losing my hearing. Kids are smart, and they figured out my hearing loss before the teachers or even my parents did. They would ask me to guess what they were saying by reading their lips. If I guessed wrong, they would laugh at me and push me out of the way and then behave as if I didn't exist.

I became isolated and quiet. But I didn't cry or complain. I had become that stoic Blake that my mother had told me I had become. When I was home, in familiar surroundings with all the cues I knew and keyed in on, I was happy Blake.

My hearing issues affected my studies, and my academic progress went downhill. My parents made the tough decision to send me to a private school to repeat the third grade.

At the Chandler School, one of the new teachers noticed that I was having a hard time hearing in the classroom, which my parents had not noticed. At home, I would be silent and happy Blake who watched TV a lot. Perhaps because my bedroom was downstairs, away from the rest of the family, it wasn't noticed when I had the TV on louder than many would have thought normal. This new teacher noticed my repeated pattern of staring at her intently when she was talking to the class. Whenever my teacher would give us a lecture, my whole concentration was on my teacher rather than on anything she wrote on the board. Unknowingly, I had developed my lip-reading ability and was doing my best to understand what she said.

This teacher had a conference with my parents and told them that she thought that their son had hearing problems. I wasn't deaf, she told them, but I was losing my hearing and making up for it by reading her lips. When they got home, my mother was so upset. She held my hand and sat with me, and she asked me, "Why are you silent in school with your friends . . .?" I replied with silence and hunched my shoulders to imply, "I don't know."

The teacher's observation had awoken new concerns in my mother. She wondered if my loss of hearing was her fault for agreeing to have the tonsillectomy operation. She regretted not paying closer attention to the potential side effects the doctor explained to her. But regret wasn't going to fix anything. We needed to take action.

So off we went to Huntington Memorial Hospital. I did hearing tests, and they took more X-rays of my head, and yes, the doctor concluded, I was losing my hearing.

However, the cause was not because of bad ear drums or faulty connections between the nerves and the brain. The cause was my adenoids, which had grown back and were now pressing upon my eardrums, impairing my hearing.

My parents were again worried because this time, the problem was much more severe than before. The adenoids were also so close to my brain that surgery had huge risks associated with it. And this time, my mother was listening to the risks.

The doctor told us that if the adenoids were not treated fast, I could be at risk of losing my hearing for life. Normally you could remove the adenoids, which are lymph tissues that sit in your upper airway between your nose and the back of your throat, with an operation similar to my tonsillectomy when I was six. However, these adenoids were in an area of my sinus passages behind my throat where using a scalpel might cut nerves and potentially even into my brain—risks that could be life threatening.

The doctor suggested a radical solution to cure me: Nasopharyngeal radium irradiation.

The idea behind that was to push rods tipped with radium into my nostrils and destroy the swollen adenoid tissue. There were risks and even unknowns associated with nasopharyngeal radium irradiation. Any time radioactive material is exposed to the body, there are risks. The radium could cause other damage, being so close to my brain. While the doctor explained the risks of the procedure, my parents had a stark choice: Accept those risks, or have their son be profoundly deaf for the rest of his life. They decided to take the radium option.

The treatment required three sessions a few weeks apart. The doctor would precisely position radium next to my adenoids to shrink and kill the tissue. The procedure did not require anesthesia, so I was treated in what today would be called an outpatient facility. I was told to lie back on the examination table and get as comfortable as possible. My head was not strapped down, as the tilt of my head that the doctors needed to access my nasal passageways would not be available if it was. I was told that during the procedure, I could not move my head in any way—not even a smidgen. Because I was so young and may not have the self-control needed to remain that still, my head would be held still, sometimes by the doctors, sometimes by a nurse, and sometimes by my mother.

The doctors then began the procedure by inserting long rods into my nasal cavities as they measured precisely how far they had been inserted. I remember thinking that I, like any other young person, had used my fingers to probe my nose and pick the interior crust away at times, but this was going in much further than my fingers ever had. My eyes began to water, and the feeling in my nose was uncomfortable and approaching the brink of pain. The doctors continued their insertion of the rods until the radium on the tip of the rod made contact with the adenoidal tissue they were trying to shrink. I would have to lie there for 10–15 minutes straight without moving my head, not even a twitch.

The procedure worked, and before too long, I was able to hear properly. And with my hearing restored, I became one of the brightest students at my school, thanks, in part, to my previous deafness. The skills I had learned due to poor hearing served me well, as I could listen intently to the teacher and retain the information delivered. My grades improved dramatically. I would participate in class and extracurricular activities. My teachers would praise me in the classroom and in parents' meetings.

My parents were always very proud of me. I remember when I got a medal for winning a swimming race competition, my parents celebrated it heartily. And gifted me a cute puppy, a Cocker Spaniel we called Ginny. My mother, later that night, came to my room and sat with me. She held my hands and kissed them. "You know, Blake . . . throughout this time, why I never gave up hope?" she asked me in her sugary voice. I softly said, "Because you are brave . . . or you might believe in miracles?"

She smiled and said, "No, I was never strong until I saw you . . . Going through a lot in your life and staying silent, without complaining to anyone, anything to us, not even to God . . . You behaved so wisely, Blake! You dealt with all the bullies, scolds, teacher's harsh behavior, failure, your illnesses, the agonizing treatments . . . and all the while . . . you endured everything. . . You never lost hope . . ." She gave me a warm hug. I always loved the way she hugged me. I whispered back in a low voice, "No, Mom . . . I stayed silent because I just believe in miracles!"

I finally got a skateboard when I was 10 years old. And the first time I used it, I was out in the driveway. Back then, they didn't have wheels that would go over things. They were like hard clay wheels. They weren't rubber. I hit a small pebble, and it stopped the skateboard, but my forward lean and momentum caused the ground to quickly come up to meet me. My hands shot out to break my fall, and I hurt my hand.

After the fall, my mom said, "Oh, it'll be all right." But later that night when I was in bed, my hand was swollen to twice its size and really hurting, so off to Huntington Memorial Hospital we went again. My mother was alarmed at the fat hand on a skinny kid, so she put my best bathrobe on me, and we went straight from my bed to the hospital. It took no time at all for the doctors to discover that my hand was broken. So, after aligning the bone, they put a plaster of Paris cast on my hand to hold my broken bone still for six weeks so it could heal. It wouldn't be my last broken bone or my last cast in my life, but this one was destined to be signed by all my friends. The coolness of the cast wore off quickly when we got home, and my favorite bathrobe had to be cut to get it over that cast. In some ways, the pain of losing my best bathrobe was worse than the pain in my hand.

I could hear; I was enjoying success in pee-wee little

league as a shortstop and pitcher; my grades were good; and the family was living the all-American life. And then, my father was offered a significant job improvement—to be the manager of the Lockheed International office in Hong Kong. And so our family moved from California to Hong Kong in the summer of 1965 when I was 10 years old.

Suddenly, we had sold our house and rehomed our dog with an older couple who were friends of my grandmother (and who gave Ginny a great life), and I had gone from the life of a middle-class California kid to an international life of expat privilege. For our first six weeks in Hong Kong, we lived in the Hilton hotel as my parents searched for an apartment. They eventually found one in Rose Gardens, which was halfway up the peak. We lived in spacious apartment 4A at #9 Magazine Gap Road. Our building had about a dozen other expats living in it, and it had a splendid view of the harbor. Hong Kong means "fragrant harbor" in Cantonese, and city life was centered on that harbor.

My parents enrolled my sister, Joyce, and me in a highly reputed British private school, Royden House, that was recommended by the American Embassy. At the time, the British still administered Hong Kong as a colony, and English was the language of business and many aspects of life. People spoke Cantonese, especially those refugees from China, while Mandarin was not yet as prevalent as it is today.

People in Hong Kong were wary, if not downright terrified, of Chairman Mao in China. In 1958, he launched what was called the Great Leap Forward, which aimed to change China's economy from agrarian to industrial as quickly as possible. It led to the deadliest famine in history and the deaths of 15 to 55 million people between 1958 and 1962.

A year after we landed in Hong Kong, Mao started the Cultural Revolution, which was designed to purge any "counterrevolutionary" elements from society. It lasted a decade and was marked by violence between social classes, the destruction of art and cultural artifacts, and more death. Refugees from Mao flooded Hong Kong, and while I wasn't aware of them at the time, I know now how much suffering was around me while I lived like a prince.

My mother would drive my sister and me to school at Royden House, and we would bring our lunches in our lunch boxes. Our Chinese classmates were driven to school by chauffeurs and had their lunches delivered by their amahs, or nursemaids. My feeling of privilege was relative, as there was true wealth all around us of which I had no real conception.

My father's position and American-based salary allowed us to have an amah, too, named Aha, and a "cook boy" named Wong. One day, my mother came home and saw Wong walking down the hallway to my room, bearing a silver tray with a bottle of Coke upon it. There was a bell in our kitchen that rang when you pressed a button in our room and showed Wong where to deliver your bottle of

Coke. After my mother spoke to me, that was the first and last delivery I had from the kitchen. I would fetch my own food and drink from then on.

Our school was far from ideal, a point driven home after a teacher told my sister that George Washington was a famous general but he was never the president of the United States. After that bit of unforgivable pedagogic ignorance, we started calling Royden House "Rotten House," and for the second year in Hong Kong, I was enrolled in the Hong Kong International School, a new American school. It opened in temporary quarters in Repulse Bay and then moved to a permanent building the next year. My sister went to a different private school named Maryknoll, and in our third year in Hong Kong, she joined me at the HK International School, as it now offered all the grade levels. At least at our new schools, they would know who George Washington was.

I liked school in Hong Kong, and I was good at it. I was also becoming independent. There was the Peak Tram station 300 yards from our apartment building. I would take the tram down into the city, as they didn't have subways in the three years I lived there, so I would take the Star Ferry across to Kowloon. Half a mile into Kowloon was a bowling alley, and I joined a bowling league in Hong Kong. I was 12 years old.

Hong Kong 1965

I also went to the movies by myself. Hong Kong cinemas had assigned seating, so you bought the ticket for your very own seat. *The Sound of Music* came out when I was living in Hong Kong, and I went to the theater to see it maybe 11 times. I loved the fact that Captain von Trapp and his kids beat the Nazis and kept on singing. The cinema also had dried seaweed instead of popcorn to snack on. It was an acquired taste.

I also learned to golf in Hong Kong at the Sheko Country Club out at the end of the island. The course is a little miracle, nestled into the rugged clifftops running along the coastline, with just enough space for 18 short holes, the front nine overlooking the ocean and the back nine winding around a tranquil valley.

It was a very English club, and my father became a member—and when he left Hong Kong in 1968, he paid

$50 to become a member for life. We have enjoyed going out there as members on subsequent visits back to Hong Kong. I took a couple of lessons, and my father—in the eyes of a 12-year-old—was a good golfer, but then, what dad isn't the best at everything? He was proficient enough to teach me the basics of the swing, and I had enough good hand-eye coordination to make my interest in golf grow. I developed a love for the game, one that deepened when on New Year's Day, 1967, I was there with my father to be the first group to tee off before a tournament scheduled for later that day.

The first hole was 212 yards away, and my father launched the ball, an Eagle Number One, into the air. It landed and bounced between two traps, then over another one onto the green and into the hole. It was my father's first and only hole in one.

The numbers of that day have always stuck with me: My father was the first player of the day, playing the first hole, and he was the first person to get a hole in one on that hole. He used an Eagle Number One ball, and getting a hole in one on a par three is known as an eagle. It was the first day of January and of the year, and I figured it would be a great year ahead. It was good Joss. In Hong Kong beliefs in idols and gods is very strong. The English word for the Chinese idol that confers luck is Joss. And having good Joss in one thing is thought to carry over into other aspects of your life as well. So certainly, this year would be a great year.

I see my introduction to golf not so much as the beginning

of the passion I have for it today but more as a substitute for not being able to play baseball and football and those other American sports that my contemporaries were playing back home.

So golf it was. I also enjoyed swimming in the great pool at the club, and I learned how to play bridge between the ages of 10 and 13. I was becoming a global citizen, but I don't know if I was consciously aware of that until I got back to La Cañada and compared myself to those who had not had the same experiences and were still in Suburbia USA. Here I was, living in Hong Kong, hanging out by the pool at a country club and traveling by myself to bowling leagues and movies. I was achieving the kind of self-reliance that would serve me well when I went to Beirut and to study in Heidelberg. So, while I missed some of the "classic American boyhood" of baseball and football and beach parties, I matured faster than the average guy in America.

I also learned some things about life in privileged society, as my father needed to entertain all the people who came through Hong Kong on business, as well as the local contacts who could help Lockheed's business and, by extension, the US business interests in Asia. All the visiting dignitaries, senators, and congressmen would stop by to find out what Lockheed was doing, and I would host them at our apartment. My mother would tell Wong that we had 10, 20, or as many as 50 people showing up for drinks and hors d'oeuvres, and he would set to work.

I worked, too, at some of those parties when I was 12 years old. I wore a custom-tailored red jacket—the cost of custom tailoring was about the same as buying off the rack back in the US. I tended the bar and learned to see alcohol as just part of a social scene. This, too, was valuable, as it wasn't a mystery to be binged upon or a vehicle for rebellion when I returned to the United States.

In Hong Kong, my mom collected snuff bottles, and I remember going to buy one for her birthday at a shop on Ladder Street. I was the first customer of the day, and it is considered a good Joss for the shopkeeper to make a sale to the first customer of the day. There are two prices in many cultures, one for the locals and a higher one for people like me, clearly a foreigner.

Ladder Street 1965

The snuff bottle I was looking at was quoted as costing 13 or 14 Hong Kong dollars, which was about $2 US. Knowing that I should ask for a better price and also believing that I only had $10 in my pocket, I told him that I did not want to buy it for that much. So I asked him if I could buy it for $10, which is a reduction of about 25 cents. This was probably the cheapest snuff bottle that he had on the shelf, but at this ask, the smile on his face melted to a serious face. The game was on. He said, "No, I can't do that, young man. You know, I may be able to come down to 12."

In normal negotiating, you would expect me to come up to $11, but I reached in my pocket, and I realized, unbeknownst to him, that I didn't even have $10. I only had $9 in my pocket. I said, "Well, no, really, all I can give you is nine." Instead of going up, I had gone down in my negotiating price. And he had this shocked look on his face. And he said, "Oh no, we can't do that, you know!" and we went back and forth a little bit here, and then he said, "OK, I will come down to your price of $10." I was having fun at this point, and I said, "Well, no, you didn't like my price of $10. Now I'm only willing to give you half." There was more back and forth, and I took a few steps toward the door. For only a Hong Kong dollar, he knew he could buy some good fortune for the day, so I wound up buying the snuff bottle for seven Hong Kong dollars. And I'm sure I bought it for that price because he wanted to make the first sale of the day. So it would be a good business day for him.

And maybe he let me haggle with him so successfully because a pre-teenage American boy haggling over the price of snuff bottles amused him. All I know is that my mother loved the bottle, and I felt confident that I could go into any market anywhere and come out with a good deal. I had also learned that the posted price is, many times, just a starting point. And that you probably will not get the best price unless you attempt to leave and then are brought back in by the seller. I would save a lot of money buying cars in my life because of that inexpensive snuff bottle.

When we left Hong Kong to return to California in 1968, we made a grand tour homeward, traveling through parts of Thailand and India and then visiting Athens, Rome, Paris, Amsterdam, and London. We went to Bangkok and admired images of the Buddha and took water taxis. Then we traveled on to New Delhi, where we took a day trip to Agra to see the Taj Mahal and inhaled the fragrances of curry. We had a long layover in Tehran, and when we got off the plane while it was refueled, we only saw the inside of the airport—and we felt the heat, which was intense. We stopped overnight in Beirut, which was my first encounter with souks and Arabic culture in this dusty, mixed-up city that was trying to be modern but still had ancient ways everywhere. We traveled on to Athens and stayed at Cleo's, which was recommended by the book *Europe on Five Dollars a Day*—as were a lot of the places we stayed, as we were traveling on a very limited budget.

This trip was back to middle class from the three years of expense-account privilege, but it was a grand tour, nonetheless. We saw the Parthenon in Athens, and both it and the city struck me with wonder. As I looked at the Doric columns of the Parthenon, this ancient temple on the Acropolis, one dedicated to Athena, goddess of wisdom and war, I remember thinking, "How did they have the technology to build these things 2,500 years ago? How did they do it?" I was mystified by how they could construct these majestic buildings that were still here. They didn't have power tools. And I know they had slaves, but they still needed an architectural imagination and an ability to execute it to this magnificent degree. It flooded my young mind with questions, and maybe it was even the beginning of my desire to know more about history.

I know that my adventure in history continued as we went on to Rome and took in the Colosseum and the Sistine Chapel at the Vatican; in Paris, we visited the Louvre, the Eiffel Tower, and Napoleon's tomb; we saw Rodin's *The Thinker* and the *Arc de Triomphe*. In Amsterdam, we saw the canals and Anne Frank's house.

Then we went to London, which was a medieval fantasy come to life for me because of my interest in King Arthur, the sixth-century Celtic king, and his Knights of the Round Table. I loved the fact that the stories of Arthur presented him as a benevolent king as opposed to a selfish one, and the people loved him for it. I always loved that concept, and at the time, I loved that London still had forts and Gothic churches and castles. And it had the Tower of London with its moat, which you could easily imagine the Thames River flooding, and the Beefeater guards in their red tunics and flat black hats, patrolling this tower built a thousand years ago by William the Conqueror. Everything medieval spoke to me in London.

My interest in Arthur had been sparked by the movie *Camelot*, which came out in 1967 and which I had seen in Hong Kong. I loved that movie and still do. I can probably sing every one of its songs, and in fact, part of the reason my daughter is named Vanessa is after Vanessa Redgrave, who played Arthur's queen, Guinevere.

I also fell in love with Agatha Christie in London. Well, not the person, but her play *The Mousetrap*. I saw this extremely entertaining whodunnit with a twist for the first time on that trip with my parents. I love mysteries, and this play kept me guessing and laughing and everything else that the theater can do to your mind. It was a great play, and I have now seen it almost a dozen times. Every time I go to London, which is my "decompression city" (English-speaking, with such cultural richness to offer as to get you over jet lag), I go to see *The Mousetrap*. And I am still delighted and surprised by the ending, which you will have to see to find out.

Then we took a long flight back to Los Angeles. How many 13-year-olds had been around the world on a trip like this at that point in their life in 1968? It was a trip that would carry me forward on my travels for the rest of my life.

At the time, I had no idea how one of the cities we had visited, Beirut, would come to influence my life, and really, at the same time, I had no idea how well my formative years in Hong Kong had set me up for my life in Beirut and Europe. It was all a grand adventure ahead, and I was excited to be heading back to California to begin my teenage life in the land where I was born. I didn't yet know how foreign that land would appear to me, nor I to it. But I was about to find out.

3

BACK IN CALIFORNIA

In the summer of 1968, my family and I returned to California from Hong Kong after three years in Asia, as my father was again transferred, but this time, he was transferred home. We had sold our house in La Cañada when we moved to Hong Kong, so now the choice of where to live was wide open. Palos Verdes, Toluca Lake, and La Cañada were all in the running. In the end, my parents found a house in La Cañada—the town I had known as home from 1960 to 1965. If I thought that I was going to step back into Californian life untouched by my three years in Hong Kong, I was soon to be proven wrong.

My mother had contacted some real estate agents, but every house that they thought might suit us was either out of our budget or the places were not to our taste. While we had a cook and an amah in Hong Kong, and an expense account that paid for our entertaining, a Western wage stretched farther there to create what many would call a privileged life. So the reality of American expenses hit home upon our return.

The patience of the agent was astounding as she showed my parents numerous houses. In the end, my parents decided the very first house that they had been shown was the one. It was a reality check on the economics, to be sure, and at the upper end of what my parents thought they could afford, but with help from their parents, it became our new home. The house in La Cañada was in a good neighborhood, with fine schools and, just like most of small-town America, a main boulevard with all the essentials for life. It was within commuting distance to downtown Los Angeles but had a real small-town feel. And as I mentioned, we had lived in La Cañada before.

I went to see the house with my sister and mother and the real estate agent. The one-story ranch-style house was perched a bit back from the street up a small hill covered in ivy. The walkway to the front door was of old brick that had roses between it, and the house and a dichondra lawn stretched out on the small plateau of a front yard. Brick accents and a wood shake roof completed the overall feel of understated elegance; it fit my parents beautifully.

My mother wanted a "fragrant garden," and the bones of that were already planted in the planters across the length of the house in the front yard, which already had roses blooming in the rays of sunshine that found their way through the well-established pine trees that provided additional privacy to the lot. I just wanted a place to call home, and when the real estate agent unlocked the front door, tall enough to accommodate a giraffe and certainly my six-foot-five-inch father, I stepped into a hall that bisected the formal part of the house, with the dining room on the left and formal living room on the right. All of the custom teak furniture that my father had commissioned in Hong Kong would be accommodated easily in these rooms. A few steps further through a doorway and the living space opened up and greeted you. The kitchen, breakfast room, and family room with a huge brick fireplace and 12-foot-long hearth that you could sit on all flowed together as one extended room. The glass doors looked out on three-quarters of an acre of hillside lot and pool area.

Down a hall to the right were the master and two other bedrooms and two baths. And to the left was a laundry room and an area that was once a breezeway between the house and the garage that had been converted into a bedroom and small bathroom. There was space everywhere!

My sister would have a bedroom and a bath to herself, as she was smack dab in the middle of her teenage years! The extra bedroom would become a library—it was really the first house that I lived in that had a library, although I would not realize the impact until later in life. For reading was not a pleasure sport while I was in high school or in this house; it was not until a stint in a hospital bed later in life that I would grow to enjoy my page-turning adventures into the imagination. The feel of the room was peaceful, though, and it touched me in a way that other rooms in the house, with their sounds and hecticness, could not.

I would be at the other end of the house in a room with crazy angles, a built-in desk with shelves above, a small walk-in closet, and a wall easily viewed from the bed. This wall is where I would hang a poster of the poem "If" by Rudyard Kipling.

The house was perfect, and when the purchase was complete, we moved in, fully expecting this could be a "forever home" for my family. That would not be the case, as the gypsy lifestyle of international sales at Lockheed would relocate my parents several more times in their lives—and continue to make travel an ever-present staple in our lives. But for now, we were home. And soon, reality kicked in.

One of the things one must remember is that La Cañada is located in the Los Angeles Basin, at the foothills of the Verdugo Mountains in the Crescenta Valley, in the western edge of Southern California's San Gabriel Valley. We lived there before the Air Quality Management Control District really put in measures to deal with air pollution, so the smog would get so bad in 1968 that it would be tough to breathe, and your eyes would water from the sting in the air. On some summer days, the schools would cancel football practices because the players were gasping for air, and not because of exertion. They couldn't breathe.

We lived four miles away from the mountains, and there'd be many days when you could not see those mountains because the smog was so thick. When you flew into the LA basin, you flew into brown muck. You'd be flying above it, and you'd look out, and there'd be this thick brown layer that you would descend through, one that wasn't a cloud layer. It was smog. And it was bad where we were because there was an inversion layer in the Los Angeles Basin. Sea breezes pushed the smog into the mountain areas, and the mountain areas would trap it all in the Los Angeles Basin.

We welcomed the rain, not only because we were living in a desert environment but because it cleaned the smoggy air out. And for a day or two, we would see the mountains behind Los Angeles with their gorgeous snow-peaked tips, that picture postcard view of mountains and valleys and lushness that attracted people to California. Those two or three days were fabulous. And maybe they happened 10 times a year, mostly in the winter when there was even snow on the peaks of the mountains.

Another type of reality happened as well when I entered the school system. I was supposed to enter the seventh grade, having finished the sixth grade at the Hong Kong International School. However, the La Cañada school district was unsure of the educational standards and curriculum of overseas education and decided that I should be tested to place me at the appropriate level. Having been held back in the third grade due to hearing problems, I chronologically should have been in the eighth grade. The test results came back, and skipping back up to the eight grade was what I would do. I would be in the same grade as people I had known from before Chandler when we went to Hong Kong!

The three years that I had spent living in an expat society, learning to play bridge to fill in at my mother's bridge parties when the fourth or eighth couldn't make it, learning to be a bartender for their parties, and engaging equally with the parents as with kids my own age, had matured me faster than any of my new-old friends.

I had also missed the American social pressures of rebellious smoking, drinking, or trying out the mood-altering substances available to kids at the time. As most of the social interactions revolved around sports, the three years that I had been away proved to be the formative years for team sports, when kids learned the skills and fundamentals of American football and baseball. The organized sports in Hong Kong did not include football or baseball. I was an outsider looking in.

I wasn't exactly antisocial. I was just terrible at interacting with people. I was bad at communicating and introducing myself to others. I was awful at making friends and did not do "hangouts" or go to parties.

Similarly, I was bad at dating. I remember a funny story now, but a painful experience at that time. Gigi, whom I liked so much to talk to, was my crush or, I would say, my "first love" at a young age, though I would come to revise my ideas on first love as I grew older. I somehow got her home phone number and communicated a bit, hiding my insecure self.

Whenever I would call her, I could imagine her soft hands playing with her hair as she spoke to me. She had thick, naturally curly hair that hung a little bit below her shoulders—and that was always tied in a ponytail. It was dark brown with a few caramel-colored highlights. She had honey-sweet lips that I imagined were lilac soft. I remember her laughs and giggles when we chatted. Her personality was bubbly. Gigi was probably the crush of the whole class.

So the insecure guy that I was tried to ask her out. I called her one night, and when she picked up the call, we had a nice but short conversation. In the end, we both agreed to meet at the high school football stadium at 8 a.m. sharp before school to hang out a bit.

The next morning, I woke up early and took almost 25 minutes to get ready to meet her, which was about 20 minutes longer than I took to get ready for school on any other day. I wanted to be looking my best.

When I reached the stadium, I saw Gigi and waved at her. She was looking pretty, as always. She wore a knee-length baby pink floral skirt paired with a crinkled blue shirt. Her hair was tied in a ponytail. Along with us, there were a couple of football players whom I knew, but only from a distance.

However, the thing that haunted me on that morning was that Gigi, who had agreed to meet me, making me deliriously happy, now gave me an awkward smile and ignored me as if none of our agreement had ever happened. When I reached home, I tried to call her a few times but couldn't reach her. After waiting to speak to her for the entire day, I was relieved and anxious when she finally called me. It was late, and I was asleep, but I grabbed the phone, and I turned on the lamp and sat up straight as we spoke.

Gigi's voice was low and almost bored. So after some awkward chatting, I finally asked her what the matter was. When she answered me, it felt like I was disappearing into the earth. Gigi said very rudely that she confused me with another guy named Blake, who was the crush of half of the girls in high school. When she heard "Blake" on the call, she said she thought he was calling her and had asked her out. But when she met me in person, she realized she was speaking to the wrong Blake.

After Gigi's confession, I was wretched and broken. I could barely focus on anything. I had no appetite, and I couldn't sleep. I just knew I would be the laughingstock of the group she hung with, the popular kids, from then on. One Sunday morning, I was watering flowers in our garden when my mother's friend visited our home. My mother was so happy to see Mary Gonzales, whom she had not seen for some time. They sat and had tea together. After a long meeting at lunch, Miss Mary suggested that my mother plan a day at the beach. My mother liked the idea, and we planned an outing to Mary's house in Malibu for the next weekend.

My mother, sister, and I went to Malibu but without our dad, as he was on another international business trip. We went directly to Mary Gonzales's house, which was right on the beach. The sky was a shade of teal, streaked with pearl white. I looked at the sky and out at the shimmering Pacific Ocean and the Eden-green beauty of the palm trees, lined in serried rows and inclining their heads in obedience toward the sea, and saw perfection. The sea glistened with the sunlight bouncing off it like diamonds on the water. I walked to the water's edge and reveled in the feeling of the waves lapping my legs and then receding, then returning, in an eternal rhythm.

I tried to let my Gigi-depressed soul rest that day, as I was here to savor the beach's indescribable beauty. With luck, I would carry fragments of it home as a memory. I consciously took it all in again, like my mind taking a photograph that could be stored in the album of my life. Everything felt like it came to a standstill, and the sunlight's effect made the scene look like one in a painting. The waves broke gently into white foam on the Malibu beach. The small rock crystal in the sand sparkled against the sun rays. The seagulls rode with the wind, and the soft sand cushioned my toes.

We ate different foods, drank a lot of juices, played volleyball, body surfed and didn't worry about a thing. In the end, we clicked many pictures that could fuel our memories later, in winter. Best of all was that in the home of Mary's next-door neighbors, there was a litter of cute puppies. My mother said I could have one, as I missed the dog we had left behind when we went to Hong Kong, so I picked a puppy and got it home. Perhaps more accurately, he picked me, climbing over his brothers and sisters to get to me as I leaned over to pet them all. Puppy mouth nips, his tail wagging nonstop, and happy sounds and kisses created an instant bond.

I loved his molten-brown eyes and his glossy fur. He also had the cutest little paws, like a fox's paws, and he loved to dig up the garden with them. He also had a tail that was constantly swishing back and forth, showing his obvious joy at bonding with a boy. He was a mutt with a clear Shepherd piece to his genetic puzzle. We called him Sheko after the country club where my dad had gotten his hole in one in Hong Kong! That dog was with me throughout my school life until he went to Beirut with my mom, then to Paris, and then back to southern California. In those first few months, I had had my heart broken by an adolescent crush and then mended by my first true love, a love that every young boy needs in his life, his dog.

But I still had to get through my school life, and I would lie on my bed and look at Rudyard Kipling's poem "If" that hung on my bedroom wall. It pretty much described how I believed that you were supposed to raise yourself as a gentleman, which, despite the opposition from people like Gigi, I was trying to do. Here it is, so you can see what I mean:

If you can keep your head when all about you
Are losing theirs and blaming it on you,
If you can trust yourself when all men doubt you,
But make allowance for their doubting too;
If you can wait and not be tired by waiting,
Or being lied about, don't deal in lies,
Or being hated, don't give way to hating,
And yet don't look too good, nor talk too wise:

If you can dream—and not make dreams your master;
If you can think—and not make thoughts your aim;
If you can meet with Triumph and Disaster
And treat those two impostors just the same;
If you can bear to hear the truth you've spoken
Twisted by knaves to make a trap for fools,
Or watch the things you gave your life to, broken,
And stoop and build 'em up with worn-out tools:

If you can make one heap of all your winnings
And risk it on one turn of pitch-and-toss,
And lose, and start again at your beginnings
And never breathe a word about your loss;
If you can force your heart and nerve and sinew
To serve your turn long after they are gone,
And so hold on when there is nothing in you
Except the Will which says to them: 'Hold on!'

If you can talk with crowds and keep your virtue,
Or walk with Kings—nor lose the common touch,
If neither foes nor loving friends can hurt you,
If all men count with you, but none too much;
If you can fill the unforgiving minute
With sixty seconds' worth of distance run,
Yours is the Earth and everything that's in it,
And—which is more—you'll be a Man, my son!

You can see how Kipling creates a recipe for masculine success, for keeping an even keel, or in his world, keeping a "stiff upper lip" as chaos might reign around you. It's attractive on one level, especially to a teenage boy who was isolated from his peers and reliant on himself. It assured me that I was OK. That I could make the best out of being different. It gave a certain nobility to rejection when you could rise above it.

Now, the problem with that poem is that it was written in 1896 in England, and while inspired by the unsuccessful Jameson Raid in the Boer War, it was steeped in that repressive Victorian-era character trait then seen as a virtue by the British but which made it difficult for men to express themselves emotionally. So that poem hanging on my wall also echoed my own pretty staid upbringing in Southern California, one influenced by the England of a century earlier.

So, I used that sensibility and my self-reliance to earn

money for myself. When I was 13, I worked as a gardener, and then I got my first job as a busboy at Perry Boy's Smorgasbord when I was 15 and could get a workers permit. And then I had a job as a box boy and then as a checker at Alexander's Market, so I was putting away a little cash even if I wasn't putting a lot of friends into my emotional bank.

The second year back from Hong Kong, I became a freshman in high school. I was five foot ten and weighed 98 pounds, so the basketball coach snagged me for the team and made me the center. I had not played basketball in Hong Kong, nor football, nor baseball, and now the sports I had missed playing were not only thrust right into my face, but I was expected, because I was tall for my age, to be a player. And the coach certainly thought I would fill out and keep growing, for, after all, my father was six foot five.

I never grew another inch, and so everybody else started passing me by—literally, on the gym floor. Not that I didn't give it my best effort. I could run suicides all day long, a grueling running drill where we'd sprint from a starting point to each of a series of lines across the court and back again. I could even jump up and hang on the rim. But setting a screen would see the bigger guys pushing me all over the court. And then there was the small problem that I hadn't touched a basketball before, and so the fine motor skills of getting the ball to fly through the air and drop through a ring 10 feet high were not something that came naturally.

So the coach and I decided that basketball would be

better off without me. I would try my hand at another sport. Football was out, as I didn't know what a blocking scheme was, and I didn't know plays or why people moved this way or that way on a football field. It also looked like a hell of a lot of work. And there was that issue of being so small that they wouldn't have to block me; my opponents could just run over me. I'm not lazy, but in playing the percentages, it seemed to me that football would use more of my brawn than my brain. And I didn't have any brawn. I was certainly not going to put myself through getting physically beaten up in practice to sit on a bench during games. Of course, I didn't realize, but I was soon to find out that any chance to be included in the upper crust of social life in this high school was directly connected to performance, or at least participation, in football.

By the time I was a junior, I was still five foot ten and had gained weight, so I now weighed maybe 105 pounds dripping wet. I was skinny and had failed at basketball, had never done any football or even seen the inside of a weight room, so I didn't think anything would come of our Presidential Fitness exercises in gym. We were told, "OK, you're going run for five minutes around the track. And how far you run will determine your score for Presidential Fitness. Run hard, and run as far as you can."

So the coaches started us off, and I started running. I didn't think anything about how fast to run or how to pace myself; I just ran. After all, it was only five minutes, and anyone should be able to run that long. I could swim a couple of laps under the water with one breath and tread water for 20 minutes or more, so I should have the lungs for a five-minute run. I passed a couple of guys, not realizing I had lapped them about three minutes into the run. Then the gun sounded, and the five minutes were up. I had completed more than a mile. I had run a sub-five-minute mile as a junior in high school who wasn't running track!

The cross-country coach couldn't believe what he had seen. He was also my PE coach and had also seen me run the obstacle course. And because I was so skinny and light, I set the school record for the obstacle course. It was a lot of running and a series of exercises—chin ups, step ups, the tire drill run, vaults—and then you had to sprint across the finish line. That record has been broken many times, I'm sure, but I did set it, and it stood at least until I left a little over a year later.

In one PE class, we would go and run around Devil's Gate Dam—a little over two miles. You would come back from the run and take a shower, and then you could leave gym class. So if you could run the course fast, then you could have half a period or more of free time.

I was always probably five minutes early to class. I would run the two miles, come back in, and I was already showering when some guys were just arriving late to class. I had done it all in a little over 10 minutes. Coach Logan didn't believe that I had run it because I wasn't sweating or winded because I'd already had a few minutes to recover. So he made me run it again, and I did so in about 11 or 12 minutes. Coach said I could be a world-class runner if I wanted to be, and he seriously wanted me on the cross-country team. Not that he could offer any inducements to recruit me to the team, but if he could have, I think he would have. The problem was that I didn't want to run all the time. I just didn't have the internal desire. And that's the key to success at any sport: Internal motivation and a desire to excel. As I think on it, it is that internal passion that leads to success in most endeavors. That and a lot of hard work.

So I turned to the sport I had started learning from the tennis pro who lived across the street from us. Charlie Stewart gave lessons on his tennis court, and I would shag balls for his lessons and listen to all the teaching tips he would give his students. Then, when he wasn't teaching, I would hit the shopping cart full of tennis balls as serves, pick them up and do it again. Size and bulk didn't matter in tennis, but how you thought out the game did, with your service angles and your shot placement all created to outsmart your opponent and get him to create the unforced errors that would win you points. I learned that staying in the game and being patient during a point allowed your opponent to take risks, and in doing that, they often gave up points. They could aim for the lines, and I would aim well inside them. It worked well, except against those exceptional players who actually could hit the lines regularly! And since everybody always said that

I was bright, tennis seemed like a good thing. Tennis had one other thing I liked, one-on-one competition. Having been left behind by team sports, in tennis, I could still get that feeling of achieving a competitive win.

I was on the high school tennis team, but being on the tennis team just meant your match was one of nine matches that day. And you're one point out of nine. But we were a hot tennis team, and we were beating everybody. We even beat our dreaded rivals from San Marino, who were consistently excellent, year after year. But despite it being a "team," tennis is a sport where you win or lose as an individual, so it didn't lead to me having a group of friends in high school. In fact, I remained an outsider the entire time.

Throughout my school time, I was incredibly skinny. My classmates would tease me. Sometimes they would bully me and say harsh comments like, "You look anorexic, you look like a toothpick, you would look so much better if you would just put some meat on your bones." It didn't help that once my mother had said I could have a modeling career as the image placed on Care Packages. It was a joke, but like most jokes, it had truth embedded, and it found a way into my psyche. Because of my thin body, I had developed several complexes as well. So I guess I could say that not only was I isolated, but I also tried to be isolated, as meeting new people would just ramp up my insecurities.

The closest I came to belonging to a non nerdclub like the math club, was when I got a walk-on part in *The Crucible*.

It was a minor role with one line. I learned a lot about drama and thespians that semester. And I learned that they were a social group unto themselves. But much like sports, they had been together for years, honing some skills and achieving familiarity with one another. And in their social network, new folks were seen as interlopers rather than being embraced. So my walk-on part was the beginning and end of my drama career.

When I was a junior, I had a crush on a girl named Judy. She was attractive and had long brown hair (I loved long hair and still do!) and she was one of those girls who wasn't aware, or maybe didn't care, that guys pursued her just have notches on their belt, where most of the girls were looking for relationships. I saw through the guys, and it didn't connect with me that well because I didn't participate in a relationship or get a notch on my belt. So I wrote Judy a poem to warn her about these guys that were trying to date her.

Judy 1972

A Hell Broke loose inside.
Heaven from the mind, I Confide

May this verse be unterse
Coming from strain
Pain

Yet

Hell broke loose inside
Heaven from the mind, I confide

Their will up a hill points too far
To star
Impressed maybe, sad if it be
All little they know
They show

Why

Hell broke loose inside
Heaven from the mind, I confide

To all ends infamy tends
Coming from chivalry, pilfery
A con, no: a line, fine
To win is to sin
To lose, to lose

Firm

Hell broke loose inside
Heaven from the mind, I confide

69

Lumped as one, sun and son
Free from harm
Warm
Be you careful always watchful
He Choose son, you sun

When to be fell, pick him well
Or it will be Hell
All

Heaven from the mind
Count on those who pose
Slow.

And even though I wrote it with all my heart, I never sent it to her.

I had grown use to being outside of the cliques in high school and outside of the established social order, and the fact that I didn't excel in any American sports and wasn't interested in bingeing on drugs or booze (I had tended bar at my parents' cocktail parties in Hong Kong—I didn't need to score beer with teenagers) furthered my isolation. No one even understood what bidding a short club in bridge meant or wanted to talk about my Ladder Street snuff bottle negotiating exploits or any of the other foreign experiences I had. They were just that—foreign to them—and as such, they either didn't want to talk about them or perhaps thought I was being superior. I didn't feel punished. I just knew that I wasn't a natural part of what was before me, and I accepted that.

For the most part. It also fueled my desire to graduate early from high school. I wanted to taste college life, so I applied to different schools to see if I could graduate early and go to college or whether I would have to wait until September to go to college. The whole idea behind graduating early was I was bored with high school socially. It didn't hurt that I was dating a senior as a junior and wanted to potentially "catch up" with her.

Cathy was a nice girl whom I met when I worked in the student store. She came there and got a Slushie, and she kept coming back. We would have longer conversations, and eventually, we decided that we'd have lunch together. One thing sort of led to another, and over the course of my junior and her senior year, we got to know each other. We went to some movies together and so forth. Not to be crude, but second base was as far as I got with Cathy in our exploration of our sexual beings. I'm sure there were a lot of people in the other Blake's group that were shacking up.

So, I wanted to get out of high school early, and I applied to USC and to Pepperdine. USC accepted me conditionally, which meant that the condition was my grades had to be at a certain level during my first semester at USC, or else my admission to USC would be revoked. Pepperdine accepted me unconditionally.

So it really wasn't a choice, but I wanted to attend a smaller school in Malibu where I'd had such a lovely day once upon a time, as Pepperdine had just moved there from downtown Los Angeles. Pepperdine also had three semesters a year. So if you wanted to graduate from college early, you could take three semesters a year and graduate in less than three years. I didn't want to be out of college early, particularly, but I did like that flexibility. And I really liked the idea of having a semester off every year, where I could have a long summer vacation and could do things. I didn't know what I would do with it. But it just appealed to me.

Inadvertently, I also did my father a solid. He'd been offered a promotion to head up Lockheed in the Middle East, but he thought he would have to delay until I was clear of high school, as he didn't want to leave my mother behind. My decision to graduate early freed him and my mother to head off to a new life of adventure in Beirut. Little did I know that it would soon be the city where I would have my own life-changing kind of adventure.

So as I was in my last semester of high school, which would have run from September 1972 to January 1973, my parents put our house on the market, and it wound up selling very fast. The closing date fell after they had moved to Beirut, so I stayed in the house and did the closing and the escrow for them, just making sure that the house was OK.

"Escrow" refers to a financial process, generally referred

to as an account, where a neutral third party attends to all the legal requirements and stipulations in a contract on behalf of two parties engaged in a transaction. With an escrow account, the funds are held by the third party until the transaction is complete or a contract is fulfilled. There are inspections to facilitate and some documents to be signed at the end of the escrow. With my parents in Beirut, I was given power of attorney to complete what was needed to close the escrow on their behalf. It was my first escrow, and it showed my maturity level that my parents trusted me to finish up the closing on our primary residence.

And I did so alone in a house without any furniture, as the house had been packed up and shipped into storage. I had a sleeping bag and one of those two-cubic-feet dorm refrigerators in the kitchen, and that's what I lived with for about three weeks as I finished up high school. And then they left me their car, a 1969 Cougar.

So everything was shut down, and I thought the house needed a farewell party. So I had one. I invited the drama club after my stunning walk-on role after the last performance of the play. They jumped at the chance to come to an unsupervised party in an empty house. We got a good two hours in before one of my parents' friends came over at 9 p.m. and said, "Nope, you all are leaving." So my one attempt, in an empty house, to try and get in with the drama crowd, if you will, had time called early. Even so, it was fun.

And what was even more fun was knowing I was going to be a freshman at Pepperdine University in Malibu. On the edge of the Pacific Ocean, looking out on my brave new world. And I knew I would find a way to become more worldly. Pepperdine was going to launch me into my next chapter, and it was going to be glorious. Before I did that, I was going to indulge my love of travel. I was going to Beirut to see my parents and my dog and take a breath before plunging into college life.

4

BEIRUT PART ONE

When I landed in Beirut in February 1973, I was coming across the world from California to my new home in the Middle East, as my parents now lived in this ancient city, and I was a 17-year-old coming "home" after high school and before my first college semester.

I was, of course, a pretty well-traveled 17-year-old, as I had lived in Hong Kong for three years and had been to many of the world's great cities, including Beirut. I had only been to the "Paris of the Middle East" for one day, though, so now I was looking forward to getting to know the place. I figured my chances were pretty good, as I would be in the city until April.

I came to refer to Beirut as a city that straddled the 12th and 20th centuries. This urban jewel that was first settled by people more than 5,000 years ago had buildings in the central city dating from the 12th century. And right next to them would be new concrete 12-story buildings that threw shade over those vestiges of the past. My parents had an apartment in the southern part of the city in a neighborhood that had been recently developed. Their high-rise apartment building overlooked spacious undeveloped lots, and it and could have been in Southern California in many respects, except for the fact there was a Palestinian refugee camp just down the street.

The camp was called Mar Elias, and it was one of the largest and oldest Palestinian Refugee camps in existence. Mar Elias camp was founded in 1952 by the Congregation of St. Elias to host Palestine refugees from the Galilee region of Palestine. It was inhabited by mainly Christian Palestinians, as well as a large non-Palestinian population. It was two city blocks long by one block wide and bisected in the middle by Dr. Philippe Hitti Street.

My parents' apartment building was half a block to the south on the other side of Gabriel El Murr Boulevard. The entire camp had walls, at least 12 feet high, surrounding it, with the entrances to each of the two halves of the camp in the center of the street that ran through it. Buildings were wedged in tight, with multiple stories and shaky staircases. Circuitous walkways were built with no real urban plan to begin with. There was no grid, much like the entire city itself. In places, the passageways were barely wide enough to get two people going in opposite directions through them comfortably. I knew that I could look at it, but I could not enter it. It was so close, and yet it was off limits to the likes of me. My mother had gone in there once to buy some needlework, and she made it out in one piece. I knew that the Mar Elias camp was not a destination for a visiting American kid who liked to take photographs.

I loved my parents' apartment in Beirut. It was wonderful, with three bedrooms and three baths, as well as a spacious living room, dining room and kitchen. They had a maid's quarters and maid's bath and a beautiful young maid from the Seychelles whose name now escapes me, but I remember how she would set my 17-year-old hormones ablaze. Of course, I was too much of a gawky 17-year-old to say anything of substance to her, but I did like to talk to our driver, Rashid, who was in his early 30s and had a wife and a child, and who was good to me.

Of course, one of the best things about returning home was to be with my dog, Sheko. He was a 45-pound, mostly German Shepherd mutt, and he was smart as a whip. In the apartment in Beirut, we would have five different toys, hide them all over the apartment, and tell him to go fetch a specific toy. And he would search the apartment, find the toy that we had asked him to find, and bring it to us. I remember how excited I was on the ride in from the airport to see Sheko. A boy and his dog, I know, but Sheko was a great friend to me.

Blake and Sheko 1974

Mary and Sheko 1974

So there I was on my first real trip to Beirut, and though I had lived abroad, I was an American straight from Malibu, California, doing "first-world" activities. I was introduced to the Royal Golf Club of Lebanon by my father, who liked to show me the golf courses of the cities where he lived. The Royal Lebanon also had squash courts. And so I also learned to play squash, and I played golf out there as part of my activities, but you can play golf anywhere that there is a course. It wasn't Lebanon specific. So it took me a while to get into the groove of being in Beirut as a citizen and not as a visitor. Anyone can go and visit the tourist attractions in a city, but to get to know it and the city's culture, you need to get off the beaten path a bit, off the main streets, and explore a bit. Eat where the locals eat, shop where the locals shop, talk with the man on the street.

One of the social staples of the Middle East is the souk, or marketplace. The first time I went to the souks was with my mom and Rashid. Central Beirut was home to one of the oldest continuously occupied souks in the world, and it was amazing. Above the souks were the apartments of the shopkeepers, so the whole thing had a "village within a city" feel to it.

The Souk al-Tawileh, which dated from the Phoenician Period that stretched from 1500 to 300 BCE, was a long street of souks, and you could lose yourself in the shops selling gold and silver and porcelain and clothing and food. It was dazzling, with the people jostling together and the shopkeepers wooing customers and the sounds and smells of the souk all combining to make me well aware that I was a long way from Malibu.

It wasn't until later in my first tour of Beirut that I would even have the courage to go the souks by myself. But at the beginning of this visit, I wanted to get to know the place, so I settled into Beirut and started to explore the city. Rashid was a great help to me, showing me different areas of the city, acting as a translator, and making sure I didn't step into a place where trouble might be waiting.

Beirut – Rachid with wife and baby 1973

My parents eventually bought an inexpensive Austin American for our family to drive around, as my mother was very conscious about being self-sufficient and not exploiting people, and she felt we were leaning on Rashid far too much. So I used that Austin to drive myself around Beirut, and that's how I really got to know the city.

I would drive to my father's office on Rue Georges Picot, which also had fancy shops and restaurants, and I would go into those shops to explore as I became a little more adventurous. My father traveled around the region a lot for work, but when he was home, we loved to go to the Phoenician Hotel in Central Beirut for dinner, and he would often take clients there. The Phoenician had the best Caesar salad that I've ever had in the world. They built the whole salad tableside, coddling the eggs for the traditional mustard, Worcestershire sauce, wine vinegar and lemon dressing and adding the anchovies and croutons and Romaine lettuce and Parmesan cheese as you watched, and then you ate the fanciest, most exquisite Caesar salad of your life. People would go to the Phoenician just for their Caesar salad.

The Phoenician was right across the Corniche from the ocean. You could see the Mediterranean Sea from its windows, and after dinner, we'd walk along the Corniche and inhale the salty sea air. It was a wonderfully first-world introduction to a place that I now know was roiling beneath my very feet.

I was not as politically engaged or aware as I am today, and I was just awakening to my interest in history. While I knew that the Munich Olympic Games in the Summer of 1972 had been struck by terror when eight Palestinian gunmen from the Black September wing of the Palestine Liberation Organization took 11 Israeli athletes hostage, I didn't realize how close that event was to me now. Two hostages had been killed in the first moments of the break-in, and the subsequent standoff in the Olympic Village lasted for almost 18 hours. I, like most of the world, had watched it all happen on TV.

On September 5th, the Palestinians and their nine remaining hostages were moved to a military airport to board a plane bound for an unnamed Arab country. The German police botched the rescue, and all the Israeli hostages were killed—shot to death by the Palestinians. Only three Palestinians survived. They were imprisoned but released a month later in exchange for a hijacked German airliner. And the rest of this story would soon be played out in Beirut, but I did not know that in February of 1973.

As the days passed in Beirut, I started learning a little bit more about why the people staying in this camp just down the street from my parents' apartment were so angry. I had asked myself, "Why don't they assimilate into the Lebanese society and get on with it?" Of course, the answer to that was, like everything in the Middle East, complicated.

I learned about the Balfour Declaration, in which the British government in 1917 declared support for the establishment of a "national home for the Jewish people" in Palestine, then under the control of the Ottoman Empire, with whom Britain was at war. Palestine, at the time, had a small minority Jewish population, but this declaration in a letter from Britain's Foreign Secretary Arthur Balfour to Lord Rothschild, a leader of the British Jewish community, one subsequently published in the newspapers, made it clear that things in Palestine were going to change.

Even though the population of Palestine was, in the early 20th century, about 95% Palestinian and 5% Jewish, the Zionists argued that there needed to be a homeland, a safe place for the Jewish people. They had a historical tie to Palestine because that's where Jerusalem was, and it was once the center of Jewish religious life, with the First and Second Temples. When the Romans defeated the Jewish warrior Simon bar Kokbah in the second century CE (whom some believed to be the true Messiah, as he fought the occupying forces), the Jews were expelled from Judea and Samaria, and the Roman emperor Hadrian renamed the land after the Jews' historical enemies, the Philistines. But he used the Latin construct, and so the land became known Palaestina, or Palestine. But to the Zionists, it had always been Eretz Israel, and they put forth a compelling reason for why their new homeland should be their old one.

The colonial powers of the time, England and France and even the United States, all agreed on the Zionist principle. And from that point forward, the Palestinians were on their way out, so when Israel was created in 1948, the Palestinians no longer had a land where they could form a country.

The Palestinians called it the *Nakba*, or the "catastrophe," as this new country took away their hope for being able to remain dominant in their ancient homeland. And so they took refuge in Jordan, Syria, and Lebanon, with nearly half a million Palestinians making up Lebanon's 6.8 million citizens—with citizenship being something that the Palestinians did not have.

During that spring of 1973, I didn't hear anyone in the expat community speaking of the Palestinian problem and what might happen if an armed and angry people decided to fight back against Israel, Lebanon, or anyone in their way. I mean, they were fighting back through means that we called terrorism and they did not, but none of it made a ripple in the world in which I lived.

I was living life as part of a family abroad, and even more so when my sister Joyce came to visit with her fiancé, Reid. Joyce was three years older than me and attending Occidental College in Los Angeles, a small liberal arts college, as was Reid. They had come to "do the Middle East" on their spring break for two weeks on a not-quite-grand tour, and so we left Beirut to take a few daytrips.

Joyce and Reid had gotten engaged in December 1972. Reid was in Beirut for a little over a week, and he had to return to Los Angeles for both work and graduate studies he was doing. Joyce stayed on for a bit longer.

After Reid had left, my father's driver, Rachid, acted as our tour guide, and we took the company Mercedes and rode to Baalbek, which is about a two-hour drive northeast of Beirut. My mother loved the temples to the Roman gods Bacchus and Jupiter, and as I took in the Roman ruins, it struck me as it had in Athens that I really was a young kid in a very old place where so many had trod before me and had built such wonders. The layout of the city fascinated me to see how they had planned it and used gravity for sewage systems and aqueducts for water supply. The Roman roads allowed them to conquer the world, as it was the disruptive technology of their time.

Balbech – Family and Rachid 1973

We'd take picnics on these drives and park and eat along the way as we pleased. There were no restrictions on us, though Baalbek would later become a center of operations for Hezbollah, and you would not try to picnic under their watch.

Similarly, we could and did go to Damascus in Syria without any concern. It was a two-hour drive from Beirut, and Damascus was amazing. It was a little like Hong Kong in its mix of shops and apartments, and it had an ancient souk as well. At one end of the Damascus souk was the Umayyad Mosque—better known as the Great Mosque of Damascus. Located in the "old city" sector, it is one of the largest and oldest mosques in the world and the fourth holiest site of Islam: The mosque is believed by Muslims to be the place where the prophet Jesus will return before the End of Days and defeat al-Masih ad-Dajjal, the false prophet.

The mausoleum containing the tomb of Saladin is in a small garden by the north wall of the mosque. Saladin was the first sultan of both Egypt and Syria and the founder of the Ayyubid dynasty. He led the Muslim military campaign against the Crusader states in the Levant.

After the Muslim conquest of Damascus in 634, the mosque was built on the site where a Christian basilica dedicated to John the Baptist already stood. According to tradition, the head of the Baptist was already preserved inside the basilica. There are also three other heads of John the Baptist in Rome, Amiens, and Munich, so there's a 25% chance that this place might have the genuine head.

We were able to go into the exterior portion of the mosque but not into the interior. And it was interesting, to say the least, as it was very much like those Hollywood "Arab" movies from the '50s and '60s where you might have seen a mosque and the crowds and noise outside it, but then you go inside the walls of the mosque, and suddenly, it's quiet. On one side of the wall is holy silence, and on the other is the raucous secular hubbub of selling in the souk.

Rashid was there to help with negotiations if we wanted to buy something, but I know that we were paying more than the locals would pay for stuff. And that's just the nature of the beast. My Ladder Street experience in Hong Kong was utilized again, as the first price was just a starting point. Normally, a fair price was going to be closer to 50% of the asking price for the tourists. The souk stretched onward through the Old City from the basilica, and you could buy anything you wanted (again, anything that was legal). My parents would pick up things that were representative of the places where they had lived outside the United States. In Hong Kong, my mom collected snuff bottles, and we had some teak furniture made.

When we went to Damascus, the brass and copper pots gleaming in the souk spoke to us of the Middle East. Funny story, but on another trip, my mother bought copper and brass pieces back from Damascus to Beirut and got them past the Lebanese border guard by telling him she hadn't bought a thing. It is humbling to me now to think of how both those places that I once loved, Beirut and Damascus, have suffered so much death and destruction because of mindless war.

Joyce and Reid were very much tourists, while I was

becoming a Beiruti, at least in my own mind. Shortly before Reid left for California, my father took us all to the Casino du Liban, where all of the ritzy people of Lebanon go. It opened in 1959, and in the 1960s, stars like Elizabeth Taylor and David Niven visited Lebanon's only casino, which was perched on a hilltop precipice overlooking the Mediterranean in Maameltein, Jounieh, about 12 miles north of Beirut.

To me, it was the kind of place where you might see James Bond cruising past the 400 slot machines and 60 gaming tables on his way to the showroom, nightclub, theater, and any one of five restaurants where he could sidle up to the bar and have his shaken, not stirred, vodka martini.

On the night we were there, my father gave us each $100 (about $667 today) to test our luck at the Casino. The agreement we made with him was that once we had exhausted the cash, we'd go home. My sister couldn't bring herself to make a bet; she couldn't bring herself to do anything because she would lose money. She was not a gambler. So she just watched Reid.

I was a game player. When we were in California, I would beat all the adults at double solitaire, triple solitaire, and so forth. I would almost always win at gin rummy—in fact, I later won a leather coat from my mother playing her at gin rummy in Ankara. I was quick with numbers and quick with cards. We would play lots of card games, and I would incessantly win, which made my sister irritated. And my mom said that my worst problem in my youth was learning how to be a good winner. I would gloat, "I beat you again" as opposed to "thanks for the game." I had to learn how to be a good winner, and I didn't learn that until I was probably out of high school. It may have been one of the reasons I didn't have any close friends.

I took the $100 from my father at the Casino du Liban, and I played game after game. I played roulette. I played craps. I played blackjack. Two hours of play, and I still hadn't lost my $100. At one point, I was up to $200. And this was when you could play blackjack for $1 a hand. But I kept going and going. I lasted two and a half hours on the 100 bucks before I lost it. The problem with my father's idea was that I was pretty good at gambling. My sister was not going to play in the game, Reid hit some bad luck, and my mother lost her "entertainment" money pretty quickly, and they were soon broke, but I was on a roll.

Until I wasn't, and the house, with the odds always in its favor, eventually took the $100 from me. The funny part of that loss is that my father lost another $400 while waiting for me to lose my $100.

I stayed in Beirut until April, feeling that I had learned a little bit about myself in Beirut. I knew that I could get along anywhere, but I also knew how important it was to be close to family, to the people you loved and who loved you, and that you are never alone when you have family.

As it happened, my sister married Reid that same

September in a chapel at Occidental College, and my parents came back for their wedding. It was a little strange to be a family again in the United States. Alas, I knew it was only temporary. We had the reception at the Oakmont Country Club in North Glendale, and the thing about that wedding I remember most is the fact that I forgot my socks. So I was wearing patent leather shoes. Fortunately, the pant legs of my tuxedo rode over the top of my shoes, so nobody realized I wasn't wearing socks. It was not yet a style statement.

Joyce and Reid are still married and have two kids. Who knew at the time? Not me. I was thinking only of the days ahead. I had no idea of what would happen to Beirut or that my parents would wind up living in Paris, Ankara, Bahrain, Jeddah, and Brussels in the future and that this time next year, I would be heading off to study in Heidelberg.

There was no war in Lebanon at that point. There were local skirmishes between this group and that, but nothing that spoke of real trouble, the kind that would soon nearly destroy the city and the fabric of Lebanese life. There was no upheaval for expats. Everything was beautiful. Idyllic Mediterranean weather and food; it was the good life. So I left Beirut and went off to Pepperdine, where I would learn things as a college freshman that I had not counted on: I had to learn to be with myself if I wanted to be anywhere in this world.

5

PEPPERDINE MALIBU

I began as a freshman at Pepperdine in April 1973. The university was not yet known as Surfer U (as it is sometimes called today by the jealous), as it had just moved from central Los Angeles and was now about an hour's drive out to Malibu. It was, and is, a stunningly beautiful campus, 830 acres nestled in the foothills of the Santa Monica Mountains, with a splendid view of the Pacific Ocean stretching out forever below. I thought that it was a walk to the beach from the campus when I enrolled, but Pepperdine is up on a hill, and you need a bus or a car to get down to swim or surf or dive or just hang out. I still had my parents' 1969 Cougar and would drive along the winding seashore up to Zuma beach or drive the snaking road into the valley, taking in the stunning beauty of Malibu Canyon.

Pepperdine is affiliated with the Church of Christ, but I was not, and religion was not the reason I was at this university. I was raised and confirmed as an Episcopalian, and I went to Sunday school between the ages of five and ten. When we moved to Hong Kong, our churchgoing pretty much stopped, so when we came back to the United States, I did not attend Sunday school or religious services, except maybe on major holidays at All Saints Episcopal Church in Pasadena. I did, however, take confirmation classes at St. George's church in La Cañada, which was useful, as that document would be needed in order to be able to prove that I was a Christian. My father was traveling to the Middle East during my time in high school, and if there was to be any chance of ever visiting any of the Muslim countries, I would need a letter from a Christian church proving that I was a Christian. The reason for that was that Jewish people could not get visas to many of the Muslim countries, so you had to essentially have a document to produce at border control stating that you were not Jewish.

Pepperdine appealed to me not only because of its location but also because its semester system let me go through college faster and still have long summers to myself. I moved into Dorm 17, which featured five suites of four double rooms with a central reception lounge and shared bathrooms. I managed to get one of these rooms all to myself by simply asking for this on my housing application. It's funny how that works. Somewhere along the way, I had learned that if you don't ask, they can't say yes. If you don't ask, then you already got a no, so why not ask? It is amazing how many times you will get a yes.

Pepperdine's religious affiliation made it a very

conservative place—with no dancing, drinking, or having the opposite sex in your room, all the things any young guy would want to do when spreading his wings out from under the family roof for the first time. We wondered if dancing was really the gateway to premarital sex as the rule makers thought or what harm there was to actually spending time studying in a girl's room. But the Lord is not the only one who works in mysterious ways; it seems the devil does too!

Everybody had to attend chapel at Pepperdine twice a week, and they took attendance. While the beautiful chapel that you can see from the highway, with its stunning stained-glass windows, was under construction the first year the campus was open in Malibu, chapel was held in the cafeteria. We sang songs and said prayers, and it was like a mini-church service.

There were some on campus who were not quite Bible-thumpers, but Jesus led the way in just about every aspect of their lives. They were not trying to be missionaries on campus to convert everybody to the Church of Christ. It was an open campus as far as that was concerned. And there was no religious pressure to be a Church of Christ member. But the conservative values that the Church of Christ had were all throughout the bylaws of the school and the rules and the student handbook. And to graduate from Pepperdine, you had to take two classes in religion. As I would later change colleges and not graduate from Pepperdine, I did take one religion class on the Gospel of John while in Germany. It's the last Gospel and the one where Christianity has definitely, in John's harsh view of the Jews, separated itself from the strand of Judaism that it once was.

When I landed at Pepperdine, I was very much the person I was in high school, feeling that I didn't fit in. I had become use to being outside of the cliques in high school and outside the established social groups. So when I got into my first semester of Pepperdine, I sort of continued to be independent of the other groups. But I also realized that everyone coming to college would be finding new friends and forming their own social pods. It was a reset in many ways for everyone. However, starting in the third trimester of the school year, many of the people I was now meeting had already had two semesters together. It wasn't until the fall semester that I got my "reset" with the entering freshmen. It's funny to think about now, but one of the likely reasons that I got accepted into Pepperdine was because I applied to enter in the third trimester and not the first. Colleges have different views of the shifting student body for each semester, and what made me attractive to them in April might not have worked out for me had I wanted to start in September.

That wasn't something that was on my mind as I navigated the social landscape before me. And I decided that one way in might be through sports.

I thought I was a decent tennis player, so I went down to Firestone Fieldhouse to check out the action on the tennis courts. Pepperdine was a tennis school, and I played tennis, so why not go and check out the team? Let's say it was close to a religious experience, as the scales fell from my eyes when I saw the caliber of the people playing on those Pepperdine courts. These guys had been recruited from all over the world to the university to play tennis. They were leagues better than me. Heck, they were playing a different game. So any thoughts of playing competitive college tennis went right out the window on the strength of that one visit.

Instead, and surprisingly to many, I devoted myself to my studies and actually made the dean's list. Not only did I attend all of the classes, but I read all the books. I excelled in my child psychology and English classes that first trimester, and I was still "learning" Malibu. I was still just 17 years old.

When I went to Pepperdine, my dad paid the tuition. But I applied for whatever financial aid I could get. I didn't qualify for anything academically, and I wasn't doing anything in sports. And I wasn't personally taking out any loans. So the only thing I could qualify for was work study. So I got a job as a supervisor in the student rec center three nights a week, basically checking out ping-pong paddles and pool cues and things like that. I would do a bit of cleaning, and I would make sure that the rec room was not being abused. It was right next to the campus café, which was closed during my night shift, so things were pretty quiet.

The idea was you were supposed to have a campus job where you could actually read and do studious things while you were getting paid, but I didn't read that much at all at that point in my life. So I learned how to play pool. I worked the 7 p.m. to 11 p.m. shift, minimum wage, but it paid for my personal living expenses. Right. And nobody came in. I mean, it was dead. Occasionally, some of the basketball players who were from the inner city would come in and play pool late during my shift. And I would play pool with them.

One of the things that I did to occupy myself when I was traveling was I would go out and take photos. I had a good Minolta single-lens reflex camera with four different lenses. At Pepperdine, I took a photography class that was part of the college newspaper. Any photos that you took on campus could potentially be used in the college newspaper, which came out every other week.

I learned how to develop film and use a darkroom—skills that have gone the way of the dinosaur in our digital age. More importantly, I learned about scene construction, focal length, film speed, aperture settings, and how to create interest in a three-dimensional scene with a product that came out as a two-dimensional image. My relationship with photography went from mere interest to fascination. I passed the class with no problem, and I learned that having true interest in anything made the learning exciting rather than a chore. And I didn't mind the attention from the byline under the photos that were published in *The Graphic*.

Pepperdine believed that physical education was part of

the required coursework for every student. They offered both the routine and the fascinating as ways to fulfill that requirement. My first semester, I took bike riding, and we would cruise Pacific Coast Highway from Malibu to Santa Monica once a week. How can anyone not love cruising along next to the Pacific Ocean and smelling the salt air, watching the gulls float above you, and feeling the warm California sun baking you with its touch? The 26-mile round trip became a joy rather than exercise.

The first semester I was at Pepperdine, there were only two or three people that I got to know. They were upperclassmen who knew just how to get around the rules, for, after all, it is in the nature of many of us to push back on the status quo. So at a conservative school, you pushed the edge of the envelope to exercise those rebellious muscles, or at least, I did. I might have been considered the rule breaker among all the people in the suite, pushing the edges not to be unduly provocative but to test the limits and, let's face it, just have some fun.

If you wanted to drink, you had to go off campus. So we would go down to the local pizza place and have beers there. Or we would go to a house that somebody had access to in Malibu and have parties there. And, of course, I had that steamer trunk full of booze in my room. So, I had contraband inside my room, which, if the Pepperdine authorities had discovered it, I am sure now would have had me expelled. It was a risk I took.

A bit of my rule-breaking consisted of having visitors to my room. It was forbidden to have girls in guys' rooms and vice versa, and you couldn't have large gatherings in your room. Or really, any visitors at all for any length of time. There was a central living room downstairs in the dorms where you could meet and greet with the opposite sex. But that was obviously a public place and not a place to study or have private conversations. A student's room was private, and who knows what could go on in that privacy? After all, this was Church of Christ School, which was very conservative. They didn't even allow dancing on campus. Because we all know what dancing leads to—the fall of Christian civilization.

A few guys, maybe two or three, would come to my suite, and we would share a few drinks in my room. We didn't let everybody in the world know about it, as it was against the rules, as I mentioned. I could get kicked out, and they could get kicked out with me. There was an incentive to stay quiet. I did not want to get kicked out, but I did want to establish my own identity.

As far as my own identity went, that was something I was starting to consider. My first semester at Pepperdine was the first time I was introspective. Until then, I had just been rolling along in life in many respects, taking whatever came along as if I was watching a movie, in a way, and this was the first time I ever thought about me. I didn't have close friends that I would have heartfelt discussions with, and so, in truth, this introspection happened because I was lonely.

I turned to writing poetry because Sheko wasn't there to be my therapist, and I had always written poetry when I had something to say and I would work it out. I was never brave enough to say what I would say in a poem out loud to someone, but I could write it and express it, and even if only I knew, it brought consolation.

In fact, at emotionally difficult times in my life, I would turn to writing to clarify things in my mind and to get through the difficult time I was experiencing. I didn't journal in high school—that was what my dog was for, to talk out my troubles and share my day with Sheko, who would listen quietly and just be there for me. My dog was my journal.

It finally landed on me during my freshman year that no one gets out alive from this thing called life. I would sit on the hillside overlooking the Pacific Ocean and watch the sun rise or set and just feel the weight of life. I was not suicidal. I was just struck by the weight of mortality and my own place in it. All of life was before me, and what was I going to do?

So I started to write poems about it, and one of my poems got published in an annual creative writing publication edited and produced by the English department at Pepperdine.

Untimely End

The wind blowing at my back briskly
I look to the horizon, searching
An Island set in the eerie morning light

The layered clouds rise, move on silently
In the background I hear someone calling
With the majesty of a new day's light

Dew drops on the grass, melting slowly
Trees swaying, flowers opening, birds singing
Something unknown blocks it all from sight

On such a beautiful morning begun, barely
With the sun given life to all it touches
This stranger came and took me away.

I know that looking back, it now might suggest I wanted to be taken away from life, but I did not. I knew that there were reasons to continue living and to live well and that you had to find them for yourself. Finding that passion that defines you is so important. I didn't have mine yet.

If there's a life lesson to be learned in all of this, it's that you have to learn to be with yourself. And if you're good with yourself, you're good with the world. We all come to that realization at different times in our lives. Some of us are dropped into the deep end of the pool, and we must learn this life lesson suddenly because of intense life events. For some of us, it's a natural progression. College is a great transitional place for people to find themselves in their independence and see that this point is really when their own life starts. And rather than being scared of it, people should probably consciously embrace it more.

Even so, I was happy at each big break in the school schedule so I could escape, and at the end of my freshman semester, I felt the need to get far from Malibu. My father's contract allowed for me to fly to school from home twice a year, and home was wherever in the world my parents were. I decided that I would go back to Beirut after my first semester at college. I had been there between the end of my high school semester and the start of the first trimester at Pepperdine in April. Now I would go back again three months later to do a little comparison between Malibu and the Middle East.

My first semester had its successes and thrills and some disappointments as well. Life is like that, I was learning. And while since the age of six, I had been in my own room and separated within our houses from the rest of the family, I found out what being alone truly was all about at Pepperdine. I had come out on the other side of that; as I flew off to see my family, I knew that I was a changed teenager.

That summer in Beirut deepened my sense of the city, and now, travel was a comfortable and reliable part of my life. Not much happened that summer in Beirut, save for the fact that I turned 18 in August and could now do all the things that being the age of majority allowed me to do.

I also learned on my return that shortly after I left Beirut to begin my life at Pepperdine, things had heated up. And the Israelis had caught up with three of the leaders of the Palestinian terrorists in Beirut just after I left in April. The Israelis had found some of the perpetrators of the Munich Olympics massacre of Israeli athletes.

The 1973 Israeli raid on Lebanon (known as Operation Spring of Youth) took place in early April, when Israeli army special forces units attacked several Palestine Liberation Organization targets in Beirut and Sidon, Lebanon. The Israelis were after, among others, Muhammad Youssef al-Najja, who was an operations leader in Black September, the group responsible for the 1972 Munich Massacre.

He lived with a couple of the other targets in a pair of seven-story buildings in the neighborhood of Verdun in West Beirut, which was about a five-minute drive from my parents' apartment. It was a pretty swank area, which was popular with expats, especially British and Italians.

The Israeli operation in April 1973 was thought to have been part of a larger operation called Wrath of God, which, as the name might suggest, was Israel's intense retaliation for the massacre at the Munich Summer Olympics. It has been dramatized in TV shows and movies, particularly in Steven Spielberg's film *Munich*, and it's easy to see why. There was incredible drama and boldness to the Israeli plan of attack.

The Israeli commandos landed on Beirut's beaches from speedboats launched from missile boats offshore. Mossad (Israeli intelligence) agents awaited the commandos on the beaches with rental cars and then drove the commandos—all men—who were dressed as civilians, with some of them dressed as women, to their targets.

Three commando teams entered the buildings in Verdun and planted explosive fuses at the apartment doors of their targets while a backup team watched outside for PLO reinforcements to show up or for Lebanese Internal Security Forces Gendarmerie units to answer the sound of what was about to happen. When the fuses exploded, the commandos stormed the apartments, shooting dead their targets and seizing whatever PLO documents they could. They also killed the wife of one of the targets, as well as an elderly Italian woman who had come to check out the noise and got caught in the firestorm.

At the same time as this attack was happening inside the building, the backup team outside engaged in a firefight with a few dozen Lebanese Internal Security Forces gendarmes and PLO reinforcements. Two Lebanese policemen were killed. The commandos fought their way past their attackers and drove back to the beach, where they hopped into Zodiacs and returned to the missile boats.

While this assault raged in Verdun, another 14 Israeli commandos raided a multi-story building that housed members of the Popular Front for the Liberation of Palestine (PFLP) in another section of Beirut. The team was also disguised as civilians, and the 100 PFLP militants guarding the building fought back. Teams of Palestinian gunmen on the building's upper floors tried to take the elevators to the ground floor to fight the Israelis, but the commandos were waiting for them every time the elevator doors opened on the ground floor and killed them on sight. The commandos then blew up the building, causing part of it to collapse, and escaped by Israeli Air Force helicopters.

And while all this was happening, two other teams of Israeli commandos attacked the PLO headquarters for Gaza operations in south Beirut. A third force of 13 naval commandos landed in north Beirut and destroyed a small PLO explosives workshop, while another paratroop unit raided and destroyed the PLO's main garage, located just south of Sidon, which is about a 40-minute drive down the coast from Beirut.

As you can imagine, there were consequences, and they would eventually affect me. More than a quarter of a million people—10% of the country's population at the time—came out for the funerals in Beirut for the dead Palestinian leaders, and after two weeks of fighting between the Lebanese army and the Palestinians, the army had to admit that they could not adequately defend the Palestinians, and so the Palestinians were allowed to openly bring in heavy weapons and militarize their camps. And before too long, I would cross into the line of fire.

But I wasn't thinking about the dangers that were coming to a boil in Beirut as I returned to Malibu for my second trimester at Pepperdine in September 1973. I came back to college with the confidence that I could build on what I had achieved. I had proven in the first semester that I could do college work at a high standard, as I had made the dean's list. I didn't need to prove anything more about that.

And I was returning as a freshman with a trimester of knowledge about the campus and how it all worked. The other members of a more crowded campus in the September trimester who were freshmen and going to orientation did not have that same experience. So I was in the nice position of being a bit ahead of the game. Now I was going to try to enjoy the other aspects of college life—the last years of irresponsibility in a person's life! And who knew that he had things to accomplish. Like graduating college as fast as I could and getting out there into the world to see what I could make of it.

As people were moving into my dorm, a big burly guy who looked like a football player (he had been) came to my room to introduce himself. His name was Stu Russell. I sized him up in some conversation first, then invited him in and asked him the essential question: "Are you Church of Christ?"

It was my way of asking this guy Stu if he was one of the strict, by-the-rules religious zealots. Stu said no, he was not, and at that moment, an instant bond was created, and we had a discussion about the restrictive nature of some of the rules. Knowing he was safe, we went into my room, and I opened an old steamer trunk that I had converted into a liquor cabinet. While shared experiences lead to making friends, sharing a secret stash of booze—one that could get me kicked out—had a way of doing that as well. Stu and I became fast friends, and we still are today.

Stuart 1974

But even for all my rule-bending, I wanted to belong to a group or to be part of a group. I focused on sports because sports at Pepperdine were a pretty big deal. One sports star on campus was a guy named Byrd Everett. I knew him a bit because he used to come in a play pool late during my shift as the student rec center supervisor. He was exciting to watch play—both at pool and on the basketball court. That year, he was the leading scorer in the nation. Obviously recruited for the basketball talent he had, he was getting a good education and had parlayed his shooting prowess into a ticket out of the inner city. And, of course, you're not supposed to have any money or anything like that as a student athlete, but somehow, he drove around in a brand-new Corvette.

I wanted to be part of that high-octane world. However, I didn't have any athletic talents in my resume that would let me play in the same leagues as guys like Byrd Everett. I had already seen that reality by watching the Pepperdine tennis players bash balls around, and they were far better than I was on my best day. And tennis was my sport. So, sports were out.

Cheerleading, however, was not. Pepperdine had these tryouts for cheerleaders to support the sports teams, and to my surprise, they had no males trying out—and they needed guys on the squad. So I said to myself, "You know, I could be a cheerleader at a major university. This is cool." And we all know that the cheerleaders have access to all the

107

hot babes!

It seemed like a cheerleading slam dunk to me. So I went down and applied and got a cheerleading audition. My friend Stu had been a football player in high school. He was a guard, and he destroyed his knee, so he couldn't play football anymore. But he'd seen enough cheerleading and been a participant in the sports social environment so he would know what they were looking for, and when he saw me trying to figure out some of the cheer movements, he offered to help me.

I suggested that he sign up to go to the cheerleading trials to help me out. He did, and in the irony of ironies, he got a cheerleading spot, and I did not. He was better because he was more "rah, rah," and he was actually more athletic than I was. After all, he could actually do some of the lifts with the girls, and I was still this guy that was five foot ten and weighed 105 pounds dripping wet. So, I did not become a cheerleader at Pepperdine. I asked, but this time got a no.

I kept active with my photography, and it led to a famous photograph, and to romance. I was the photographer who took a classic photo of the singer Pat Boone. The campus had become a favorite backdrop for the movie and television industry, and Pat was there filming a commercial for the California milk industry. While taking a break from some of the filming, I saw that he was actually drinking some milk out of a milk carton. Pat Boone had his strong Christian faith and was known for his "wholesomeness," and so when he saw me with my camera, he raised this container of milk that he was drinking from as a kind of toast. Click, and the moment was captured. It's a great picture, and it got published in *The Graphic*, the campus newspaper I had been working with since my first trimester.

One of the best things that happened to me because of photography also came during my second tour of duty at Pepperdine, and that was meeting Cheryl.

She was not at Pepperdine. She was part of a mime dance troupe that came and performed at the college, and I was assigned by *The Graphic* to photograph their performance. Cheryl was skinny, like we all were, with dark hair and a nice smile, and she was a year older than me. I went up to Cheryl to ask her the names of the dancers in the group so I could identify them for the paper. And one thing led to another, and before too long, we were going on a date. And before too much longer, those dates were happening in her bed. You never forget your virgin experience!

I did not pursue Cheryl, but I walked with her down the path of romance. She lived in Pasadena, which is an hour-and-a-half car ride from Malibu, so that 1969 Cougar and I put on a few miles, and we had a long-distance, SoCal kind of romance. She was into Renaissance cosplay, and we'd go to these Renaissance fairs where everyone had to dress as if we were in the late 15th century and on their way through the narrow streets of Verona to attend a ball with the Montagues and Capulets, even though we were actually playing out the Renaissance on acres of open land in Agoura Hills in Southern California.

Cheryl and I went to that fair a few times, and we dressed up as if we were time-traveling four centuries backward. I can't even remember if I had the tights on or not, but I probably did. Cheryl really enjoyed those fairs, and I enjoyed her enjoyment and took some great pictures of her. She had this Renaissance wedding dress that was spectacular, and I took her to Descanso Gardens and had her pose on a massive rock outcropping framed by trees with the sunlight filtering through and silhouetting her body through the material of the dress, truly the look of a "Renaissance bride."

It's one of the best photos I have ever taken. And after I took it, we went back to her apartment in Pasadena, and she taught me more about two people and intimacy.

Cheryl inspired me, and I felt more connected to my own emotions. I even wrote poetry about her, and I did so in an Elizabethan voice.

Cheryl in wedding dress – Descanso Gardens 1974

Let me try to write
Though dearth to Dante
What in my heart
I know to be truth;
Observations of emotional reality.

Let me try to paint a picture
In the imagination
Of the scene painted by love

For it has come to be
That I am set free by thee
With freedom in me
I breathe joyous life.

I wear nay miter,
Nor even a cowl,
Yet I give unto you
God's Grace
The beauty of the day
To always touch
Your courtly gentleness

Clouds in the morning
Pink lips speak no lies.
The pale, blue skies
Your eyes gently persuading

The air about you sweet
Sweet as the springs after an April shower
Your smile innocent and fresh
Fresh as the dew on the morn grass

We walk as one
Through the heather
A shallop on the rill;
A hunting horn wailing,
The foxhunt in yonder dale,
The flowers all with supple corolla
Shaped of the primrose cyclamen,
Sun and eyes radiant,
Betray my feeling.

I sheathe myself in your love
A cormorant with covet for you
Impenitent I stand
Monolith fixed to requite
With regale, repartees, loving
The remembrances of the evening
Repleted with love.

There lies a coat,
A cubbyhole where,
Oblivious to all
I proceed dauntless to convey,

Covenant.

I find myself in a position
Which is foreign to me
I find myself full of emotions
I rarely see
Yet words few as these
Spoken so true
Under the breeze
Show you my view
Can you see
This is my plea

One simple sentence
Loving in content,
I wait out my sentence
To wind up content,
For music to my ears be
The gentle sweetness
Of your whispering voice.

As you can see, Cheryl had an effect on me, and I was experiencing the joys of what I thought was first love. But maybe it was really first lust. At that age, it is easy to take one for the other. We dated for a number of months, and my experience with her opened me up by using senses other than my eyes and ears to navigate the world.

Back on campus, I was making some new friends, finding a few people who shared some common interests. One of my new friends was a guy named Jeff Powell, who told me when we first met that he was going to become a dentist, and so he did. At Pepperdine, he and I both knew how to play bridge, and so we played some bridge on campus and smoked cigars, and we created dessert drinks using ice cream and sorbet and all sorts of different types of liquors. And, of course, liquor was banned at Pepperdine. So we were doing it off campus, but I still had a little stash in my room, and I could have gotten kicked out of school for that very easily. I knew that, but I wasn't going to keep all those opened bottles in the trunk of my car, so it was a line I was willing to walk.

The fall semester saw me take diving as my physical education class. And this was not diving from a springboard or platform (although they offered that as well) but under the ocean with scuba gear. This was pre-neoprene diving, so we had to wear a heavy rubber wetsuit to keep our bodies warm underwater, and our masks were designed to allow our nose to fit inside it. And it was cold down there, as once you got below the thermocline, which is the transition layer between the warmer mixed water at the surface and the cooler deep water below, you had to have a full wetsuit with booties and a hoodie!

I loved being beneath the Pacific surf, looking at the life of the sea. And catching some of it, too. My checkout dive was in open water off Santa Catalina Island, 22 miles off the California coast west of Los Angeles. Checkout dives are tests: You repeat and practice all the skills you learned during your confined water (pool) dives. The instructors check out your buoyancy and orientation to key landmarks and make sure that you have mastered everything that you have been taught before you can be let loose in the ocean on your own—well, with a buddy; you always dive with a buddy.

On my checkout dive, our instructor took two of us out and tested us. While he was putting one of us through the paces, the other one watched the proceedings. While waiting my turn at the edge of the kelp forest, I was startled by a fast-moving shape that darted past me. An instant shot of adrenaline hit my system as I thought, "Shark," and turned to see what I knew was certainly going to devour me for lunch. Instead, I found myself looking into deep dark eyes—not three feet from my facemask—staring back at me with what looked like a playful smile. It was a baby seal that had darted in and out of the kelp, and it swam past me a few more times, satisfying its own curiosity about what sort of an animal I was.

Back then, you could still catch abalone off Catalina, and during my checkout dive, I got a few to take back and eat for dinner with some friends. The dive master found some scallops as well. On the boat ride back to the mainland, he shared with us the technique of opening up the scallops and then the practice of squeezing a little lemon juice on the meat inside and eating it raw. They were a little slimy and very moist, with the consistency of a firm oyster but not nearly as slippery. The lemon accented the taste of the ocean. What a treat!

I am so glad that unlike a couple of others on the boat who were a bit squeamish, I had learned from sampling so many different flavors in Hong Kong and Beirut that you should never be afraid to be adventurous and try things. And I had one more thing to try. Upon getting back to campus and cleaning up, I was faced with a question: How do I prepare the abalone? An hour before dinner, I went to the cafeteria and into the kitchen to ask the chef what I should do. He laughed and said, "We shouldn't let you back here, but for a bite when you are done, that area of the kitchen over there is all yours." Fortunately, he also gave me instructions on how to prep the abalone meat.

When I was done, he had his bite and gave me the thumbs up. There was actually a fair amount of the tasty treat, so a few of my friends enjoyed the abalone along with the rest of the nightly fare from the buffet line. One of the not-so-fortunate students looked at the delicacy on our plates and jokingly asked, "Where did you get that? Off the bottom of the ocean?"

"Yes," was the answer.

Pepperdine was a really good place to be. There was a lot of faith and trust there, and it created a generous environment. So we didn't even think twice about going to the chef to ask if we could invade his kitchen to prepare the abalone. It's the way the place was. But again, it reinforced my belief that if you asked nicely, many times, the answer would be yes.

Though I had made the dean's list during my first semester at Pepperdine, there was no danger of that during my second. I was a very lazy student and didn't do very well academically for the next two semesters. I actually did the things you're supposed to do in college, as far as studying for my classes, going to the library, and things that ticked off the "college student" boxes. But I was still doing poorly academically because I wasn't putting in the needed work. I wasn't always going to classes. I had always gotten through academics by paying attention in classes—not going to all of them made my academic model not work.

I snuck through with a D in Western Civ, which was a huge class of 300 people that took place in the auditorium. People would take tape recorders to class so we wouldn't have to go, and often, I didn't go and didn't listen to the taped lecture, either. I got a B in English and a C in something else that escapes me now, but I do know that I had a C average.

I was interested, though, in a class in computer programming. It was a time when programming was written in ASIC, which is a subset of BASIC (Beginners' All-purpose Symbolic Instruction Code). It was created in 1964 by computer guys who wanted to open up the world of programming to the likes of people like me. I could do a little bit of programming, but I never really got into it. And so, if you didn't really get into it at the basic level, you weren't going to go on any further in programming. I had visions of grandeur that I was going to program the game Monopoly that semester, and I didn't get much past tic-tac-toe. I got a D in that class, too.

My wake-up call came when I realized that if I raised my grades, I could go study at Pepperdine's campus in Heidelberg, Germany, for a year. My friend Stu had a pal who was on a Rotary scholarship in Germany, and he alerted me to the fact that we could go to Germany, too. So, I applied for and was accepted into the program—as a sophomore. Normally, Pepperdine allowed juniors and seniors to go abroad for a year, but somehow, Stu and I both made it through.

But I still had to make it through the year at Pepperdine, and there were some close calls. Back then, I don't know if I ever thought too deeply about what the consequences of getting expelled would be, and most of the "bad" things that I did at Pepperdine were due to youthful high jinks and my own rebellious streak. It was more spur-of-the-moment things than anything pre-planned, where you could have time to think of consequences. They were things that now, in retrospect, make me ask myself, "Why the hell did I do that?"

For example, one of the high jinks that saw me on the

originating end of things happened in the spring semester. There was a baseball game that was going on on the baseball field that I could see from my dorm room. Now, this was no ordinary baseball game. It was the USC–Pepperdine alumni game.

My dorm was in a building above the baseball field, but I was a quarter of a mile away, easily. I mean, I needed binoculars to tell who was playing what position on the baseball field, as we were at least 500 feet higher than it was. Now I'm not saying that my dorm was hanging on the edge of a cliff! It was on a hill, and there was a steep downward slope between my dorm and the ball field.

As it was a fine Saturday in spring, I took the screens off my dorm windows. Then, I put my speakers from my very nice stereo system that I had bought from some of my pre-college earnings out onto the roof of the dorm, where I was going to watch the game with a couple of friends. We put some lawn chairs on the roof and sat with our shirts off watching the game. I am sure we shouldn't have been on the roof, as that was bad enough, but then I turned on the stereo.

The Pepperdine centerfielder later told me that he could hear my stereo on the field, and that was bad enough, as playing music too loud was probably against one rule or another. Making the matter worse was that I chose to play Frank Zappa's song "Billy Was a Mountain" from his album *Playground Psychotics*.

And if you're familiar with the song, it's pretty frank, to say the least. It's a 30-minute-long piece in which Zappa liberally uses "fuck" and "shit" and references un-Pepperdine species such as "lesbian queens." So it turned out that not only could the centerfielder hear the music blaring from my speakers a quarter of a mile away, but so could all the big alumni donors who had turned out for that game. I got a letter of reprimand from the president of Pepperdine for my musical participation in the Big Game, and indeed, I was very close to getting kicked out of school for that.

Another thing we did that fits in the youthful high jinks file was done to the resident adviser of our dorm. His name was David Ogilvy, and he was just a good, solid guy. He was tall and blond, with kind of a short-haired surfer guy look. He was very evenhanded. He was there to help people in emergencies and do the things required of an RA. But he didn't inject himself into everybody's lives. Right. He let the suites handle their own affairs in many respects. So he was perfect, and because it was his birthday, we thought we'd give him a birthday present.

We woke him up late at night and got him out of bed. He was in his skivvies, and we roped him to a pole like he was a captured wild boar in the jungle, and we paraded him around hanging from the pole by his feet and his arms.

It was all good fun, but then we started parading him up to the girls' dorm area. He was now objecting a little bit, saying, "Oh, come on, guys. Don't leave me here." His girlfriend lived in that dorm, and we basically left him staked in the ground out in front of the girl's dorm. And, of course, it was very embarrassing because the girl had to come out and see the RA in his skivvies, tied up in front of her dorm. And the other girls helped her untie him.

It turned out that right on the other side of the lawn from the girl's dorm lived the resident coordinator, who saw us doing this. She asked for our names during the event, and we just walked away. But I went back and came clean to her, which she acknowledged in my letter of reprimand. "It is mainly because you came to talk to me that a more stringent sanction is not being levied," wrote Glenda Campbell. Even so, I was getting awfully close to getting bounced from Pepperdine, and I knew that this was the last thing that could happen if I wanted to see Heidelberg. I have to say that Pepperdine stayed true to the values of forgiveness rather than expulsion!

There was another issue that was weighing on me as well. Because now that I was 18 years old, I had to register for the draft for the Vietnam War, which had begun in 1955 and was now, in the spring of 1974, one year away from ending. But we didn't know that then. As the war went on, selective service requirements, deferments, and exemptions changed in an effort to make the draft appear fairer. There had been a lot of poor and black and brown kids doing the fighting and the dying. There was an expression that summed up who was being sent to Vietnam that said, "If you have the dough, you don't have to go."

One of those changes was the institution of a draft lottery, which gave young men a random number between one and 366 that corresponded to their birthdays. Lower numbers were called first, and if you got called, you had to go to war. So, I had to register for the Selective Service, and when they drew the draft numbers, I just knew I was going to have a low number, that I was going to be drafted into the Army and sent to Vietnam. It wasn't until March 24th that we knew the numbers and learned that even though the numbers had been drawn, 1974 was the first year that regardless of your number, you would not be called up. So I avoided the Vietnam War because of luck, essentially. I had been born late enough to legally dodge the draft.

The fact that I was at Pepperdine could have meant that if I had been selected to go, I could have received an academic deferral. I don't know for certain that I would have received one, but my chances were good, and I knew that I would have done everything I could to stay far away from Vietnam or any war zone.

We were all aware of the conflict that the war was creating in the United States, from the Kent State shootings in May 1970 to the huge anti-war protests that happened on the Washington Mall. And the news, which you could trust back in those days, was reporting it every night, a steady drumbeat of how we were losing. Now, I had been to Beirut with a war rumbling in its air, and I had not noticed it. The Vietnam

War was not a big thing in my brain, and I registered for the Selective Service because it was what you had to do. I obeyed the law. When I found out what my number was, I was a little disappointed, but at the same time, I knew they weren't calling guys up, so I wasn't lying awake at night in fear. But it did focus me on the fact that I was in the world and had responsibilities.

That said, one of the reasons Vietnam and I were not exactly communicating on a daily basis was that I was not part of the counterculture. I missed the American drug culture experience because from the age of 10 to 13, when the first experimentation with drugs and booze and rebellion against The Man was happening, I was living in Hong Kong. I never got involved in weed or any of the culture surrounding drugs, nor was I a hippie in any way, shape, or form—save for the polka dot shirt I wore when I was 13. Heck, my idea of long hair was barely over the ear! As a result, overt anti-war messages really passed me by. I was not an activist by any stretch of anyone's imagination.

And yet, by the same token, I wasn't against activism. I wasn't anti-anything. It's just that I wasn't involved, so I didn't even think about rebelling against all the counterculture by joining the ROTC. That wasn't me. So, I missed the war by the skin of my teeth, and looking back today, I am very glad that I did.

In that spring of 1974, all that I knew was that I had now put three trimesters of Pepperdine in the books, and while having come close to being kicked out, I was still there and heading to spend summer with my parents in Beirut, then journeying off to spend a year abroad in Heidelberg. Life looked pretty good, though I had no idea that within a month's time, I would be learning about the Middle East from the back of a camel as we swept across the desert. Learning about history and how it touched me. I was about to become Blake of Arabia.

6

BLAKE OF ARABIA

I returned to Beirut in April of 1974, not so much with a swagger in my step but with more confidence in who I was then I'd had when I first landed there more than a year before. I felt as if I knew the city, and it was good to be back, to see my parents and my dog and inhale the Mediterranean air in this ancient place after the shiny newness of Pepperdine. At this point in my life, I knew that I had been infected with the travel bug, and I was glad there wasn't going to be a vaccination against it in the yellow health record booklet we used to keep track of vaccinations when we traveled internationally. Mine was a little dog-eared around the edges from being used often since 1965, when I first got cholera, typhoid, black fever, and assorted other vaccinations when we went to Hong Kong.

I had changed a lot in the year that had just passed. I had learned that I had a rebellious streak, and it had nearly seen me expelled from college for my Frank Zappa moment at the baseball game and for our "birthday prank" on our

RA of tying him to a pole in his underwear and leaving him in front of his girlfriend's dorm. In full view of an angry administrator. I mean, it wasn't major felony kind of stuff, but at a conservative Christian college, it was almost enough to send me packing.

As the days passed in Beirut, I was starting to enjoy being away from school. I spent a bit of time at the Royal Lebanon golf club. I played squash with more seriousness. I would walk the streets, exploring different areas of the city. I once walked from our apartment all the way to my dad's office just off busy Hamra Street by going down the Corniche along the ocean. It was easily five miles.

And then I got an offer I couldn't refuse. My mother was volunteering at the American Women's Club thrift shop, as she was always busy doing something. The American Women's Club was a tight-knit expat women's group in Beirut, and they organized a trip for the expat community that they called the "Camel Caravan." They had planned a camel tour of the region, and as my father couldn't go, my mother invited me to come along for the ride. I accepted with pleasure. I didn't really have a choice, as she had already signed me up!

I was one of the few males on that 42-person trek, and I was certainly the youngest. We flew to Amman, Jordan, and then from there, we hit the desert. A South African journalist, Louise Gubb, came with us, and this excerpt from her piece that appeared in *The Beirut Daily Star* on May

26th, 1974, gives you a taste of the adventure.

"Desert songs are passed back and forth between the camel drivers, and I realize that we are in another world. Far from honking services and chic boutiques, we move through a land of desert, mountains, sparse shrubs, occasional oases, and incredibly hospitable people.

This transformation of worlds happened during the American Women's Club's caravan tour of the Jordanian desert last week. Twenty-nine women and 13 men, accompanied by Bedouin guides and six journalists, visited wilderness castles, the carved stone fairyland of Petra, desert wadis, crusader fortresses and the refreshing waters of Aqaba. Six days of travel by airplane, bus, Land Rover, horseback, camel and boat provided a tour which must be seen as highly creative and successful.

Again and again we were treated to moving experiences: A small castle filled with colorful frescoes, T.E. Lawrence's fortress headquarters, the Petra treasury surrounded by blooming oleanders, Bedouin singing and dancing, a desert feast, the swaying camel journey (never mind the saddle sores). Snorkel diving among the coral, swimming off a white sand beach, underwater scenery viewed through glass bottom boats at Aqaba provided rest and play at journey's end."

From Amman, we got on a tour bus and drove through the desert to see some Crusader castles. This was the first time I'd seen anything connected to the Crusaders, who had left their imprint on this part of the world in the name of religion. The Crusaders fought in the Crusades, which were a series of religious wars in which Catholic soldiers from Europe, under the direction of the Church, traveled to the "Holy Land" between 1095 and 1291 with the aim of recovering Jerusalem and its surrounding area from Islamic rule. With the aim of recovering the "Holy Land" for Christianity.

Jordan – Crusader castles 1974

The Crusaders built these strategically situated castles along the trade and migration routes to allow for control of vast sections of geography by those who controlled the castles. Majestically situated on top of mountains overlooking the valleys below—and all who passed through them—I was in awe of the sheer magnitude of the construction process it would have taken to build these castles in the 12th century. While modern roads wind their way to the castles from the valley floor, navigating the ascent (and decent) in the days of horses and camels was surely treacherous. And sieges were the only way to possibly conquer these castles.

I started to feel history a little bit, and I would say that trip was my first exposure to being a historian, although I wasn't a real historian. I was learning that studying history was not memorizing dates, names, and places, but rather it was discovering, experiencing, and being in another time. Here in the desert, standing among the ruins of fortifications, I was just experiencing history firsthand, centuries later. But the questions I asked the tour guides were more about the past, those "why and how?" questions of history rather than the questions the normal tourist asks out of politeness. And so I wondered, as I was wandering through all of these ruins, what were they like when they were built? Who were the people living here? What were the conditions like? How were they built? Why were they situated where they were?

My imagination was in play as I explored these Crusader castles. Cheryl and I had gone to Renaissance fairs to play with the idea of how people lived in the European Renaissance. I was now trying to imagine life in these Crusader castles. For the first time in my life, I was thinking beyond just this moment. We would see how thick the castle walls were, and I imagined trying to breach them as an attacker. The castles were built on hills, with a view of the valley below, so the occupants could see any caravan that was approaching. And you could muster your horses and ride down to the caravan. Any would-be attacker had a challenge ahead of them because they couldn't attack up the hill very well, and even if you made it, you still had to bash through these tall, thick walls. The Crusader castles were very strategic—built to withstand attacks and, as I was standing in them some eight centuries later, built to endure the onslaught of time as well.

One of the castles that struck me the most was Qasr Al-Azraq, about 50 miles east of Amman. It was built by the Romans in the third century CE. Due to its location along the Wadi Sirhan trade route and its close proximity to a large lake, it was in a convenient position for the Roman military. Originally constructed from black basalt, Qasr al-Azraq was an important military base during the Byzantine period, and it was rebuilt in the early 13th century by Crusaders.

Jordan – Crusader castle Qasr al-Azraq 1974

The vast damage that we saw to Qasr Al-Azraq was not from the various sieges through time, as no army ever conquered it. The damage was from a devasting earthquake that occurred in 1837. But a lot of the castle remained. The impressive basalt door located in the western tower was made famous by T.E. Lawrence (of Arabia) in the book *Seven Pillars of Wisdom*. There was also a 13th-century mosque and the remains of a prison, along with a kitchen and dining room. Lawrence used this castle as a base of operations during World War I before attacking Damascus and securing the greater Syria that would be ruled by Arabs, as it was their army he was leading, which was first Allied army to enter Damascus. It was a momentous victory that hastened the downfall of the Ottoman Empire.

It was the tour guide who let us know that Lawrence of Arabia had used this castle as one of his staging spots during World War I. I had seen the movie with Peter O'Toole playing Lawrence of Arabia, and it captured the essence that Lawrence was a rebel. He didn't live by all the British rules. He didn't wear the British uniform all the time. He wore Arab dress. He identified with the locals, and he was an advocate for the Arabs. And I liked his character and identified with the essence of who he was.

And it was because of him that the Arab army went into Damascus before the British, kind of like the Russians entering Berlin before the Allies in World War II. Because of that action by Lawrence, the Arabs got greater Syria except for the coastal areas. The coastal areas went to the French and British, but everything other than those slivers of land along the coast that was greater Syria went to the Arabs. If the British had gone in first, it would have been France and Britain that would have carved up and controlled those areas at the expense of the Arabs.

After our visit to Qasr Al-Azraq, we wound up at a hotel outside the entrance through the mountains into Petra, where we had dinner in a very modest restaurant. Nothing fancy at all, with Formica tables and a basic menu of rice and goat. In the morning, after breakfast, we went on a horseback ride through the cracks in the mountains. We rode through a snake-like crevasse with its rose-colored sandstone walls, some 80 meters high. The crevasse was so tight that, in places, you felt that you could touch both of the crevasse walls at once.

Petra – emerging from the Siq 1974

This split in the rock is known as the Siq, and it is partly natural and partly carved by the Nabataeans, who were one of several nomadic Bedouin tribes that traveled the Arabian Desert in search of pasture and water for their herds. They became a distinct civilization and political entity between the fourth and second centuries BCE, with their kingdom centered around a loosely controlled trading network that brought considerable wealth and influence across the ancient world, and their capital city was Petra. During Hellenistic and Roman times, Petra was a major caravan center for the incense of Arabia, the silks of China, and the spices of India, a crossroads between Arabia, Egypt, and Syria-Phoenicia.

Petra 1974

The early morning light was not bright enough to shine directly down to illumine the path very well, but the horses had traveled through this rip in the mountains countless times and were surefooted. Then, as the trail emerged into the small valley tucked into the rugged mountain topography, you could see the magnificent treasury building's facade carved into the sandstone of the mountain.

It was the Nabataeans who, in about the first century CE, carved the stunning facades into the face of the red, pink, and white sandstone mountains. As the treasury building revealed itself when I emerged from the crevasse, I was overcome with a sense of awe at the artistry of the architecture and the ability to create such beauty almost 2,000 years ago. Now, all of a sudden, what man can do to create beauty if given the opportunity was coming face to face with me. I was profoundly moved that we could do something so intricate, so beautiful, carved right into the limestone of the mountain. And I was awestruck by the fact that it was still there.

It even caught the imagination of Hollywood, and Steven Spielberg used the backdrop of the treasury for his film *Indiana Jones and the Last Crusade*, the third installment of the Indiana Jones series. The American archaeologist Jones (played by Harrison Ford) and his father (played by Sean Connery) go after the Holy Grail, and then, at the end of that movie, they ride through that chasm away from the treasury building.

Petra was not conquered but rather abandoned to the desert as the trade routes shifted away from the area. The thriving city of as many as 30,000 people, with waterworks and dams that made life not so much the brown of the desert but the green of irrigation, drifted into ruin over time.

And there was a bit of humor to the majesty of the place as well. Outside of Petra, there were vendors who sold Roman coins and lamps, very old or, in some cases, very new. It was easy and funny to spot the fake Roman coins because they had BC (Before Christ, the hawkers told us!) on them after their date of minting, which would have been impossible to know at the time of production if they were real. Which they were not.

I was pointing this coin out to my mom, showing her that it was mined in "14 BC." And she was laughing, and I was laughing, and even the guy who's trying to sell us this stuff was laughing. Everybody was laughing. That was something profound that I also learned on that trip. There is an international language that everybody knows and that everyone speaks, and it's called laughter. It's the best communication there is in the world, and it can turn a tense situation into one of shared pleasure.

Petra – Bedoin Negotiation 1974

If you laugh and you have a smile on your face, it doesn't matter what you're saying. Nobody gets upset with people who are laughing. And I think that that one incident with the fake coins in Petra brought that point home to me.

After we went to Petra, we went back to the hotel and freshened up for dinner, which was going to be a "goat grab" in the Bedouin camp tents outside the hotel at the edge of the desert, which was literally 100 yards from the hotel. The local sheikh who was providing the camels for our journey the next day had a big tent that could easily hold 50 to 100 people. So we all piled in and sat down for the goat grab.

It was pretty amazing, really, when you think about it. There were all these Americans and the owners of the camels and anybody who was part of the sheikh's family all together under this sheikh's tent, enjoying a meal in the traditional Bedouin style. Dinner was a feast of goat, lamb, beef, and chicken backed by rice, raw vegetables, and a tortilla-style bread, all served on large platters. We all sat on the floor and ate with our hands, though we were told it was custom to use our left hand for eating, as the right hand was used for bodily functions and not suitable for touching food.

After dinner, some of the team went back to the hotel for a "proper" drink, which included alcohol, something which you would not be served in a Bedouin tent. Over drinks, people wondered if we should extend the tour by a day, and if we did so, did we want to take a risk and go into Jerusalem?

In the end, while people longed to visit Jerusalem, which was 200 miles northwest of Petra, the risks outweighed the benefits. If we had Israeli stamps on our passports, we couldn't get back into Arab countries. We also didn't want to upset our hosts and disrupt their timetable and make them feel they had suddenly become second-class citizens after all they had done to welcome us.

So the next day, we were all up at dawn. We loaded our suitcases into Jeeps, and then we met our camels. We were introduced to our camels by the camel drivers. After the introduction, you get on the camel, and then it rises up, and you're taught how to sit. You don't sit like on a horse: You crook your leg around the horn and then lock your other foot over it. Camels rock and roll like you're at sea, and maybe that's why they're called the ships of the desert, but all I know is that you don't want to fall off one.

Jordanian desert – Camel in morning 1974

They're tall animals, and they smell like, well, a camel. Which is to say they smell a little bit like desert and quite a bit musky. It was funny to see the reaction of some of these proper American women on the trip to being astride what they thought was an "unclean" animal. Most of them got over it pretty quickly, as they realized that they were there for the adventure and so forth. As was I. But more than that, I wanted to feel the adventure that Lawrence had felt as he galloped through the Wadis toward Aqaba.

Jordanian desert – Blake on his camel 1974

Camels have a more independent mind than a horse normally shows you. If you were in control, the camel knew you were in control, but unlike the horse, that didn't always mean that the camel would do exactly what you wanted it to do. I didn't have any problems with my camel, but some of the people did have problems, and they were riding their camels in circles, the sand swirling up around them. The camel drivers laughed among themselves at the Keystone Cops–type situation that played out in front of them. Then they stepped in and restored order and began the slow march of the caravan to the west.

Jordanian desert – Mary mounting her camel 1974

It was sunny, and it was hot, so we didn't race through the desert. We rode along in a clippity-clop fashion and kicked up desert dust as we went. You didn't want to be at the end of this Camel Caravan. You wanted to be near the front.

On this trip was an American couple, Chris and Sandy Albright, who were friends of my parents. Chris was head of Pepsi in the Middle East, and he was a very quick-witted, funny guy. And Sandy complemented him well, as she shared in the humor and was always happy. One of the camel drivers rode up to Chris and said that he wanted to buy Sandy. Chris went along with him, and I think that they were up to about a dozen camels as Sandy's selling price when Sandy stepped up and shut it down, telling her husband that he was not selling her for any number of desert ships. I think the camel driver was dead serious, but he took it in stride, so to speak, when Chris broke off negotiations.

Jordanian desert – Chris and Sandy 1974

The next day, half of our party decided that they had learned enough about camel riding, and unlike T.E. Lawrence, who surprised the Turks by attacking Aqaba from the desert on July 6th, 1917, they would enter Aqaba by Jeep. There were a few intrepid souls who rode past the hills where the fortifications had been built with the cannon facing the water and not the desert, which was one reason that accounted for Lawrence's daring victory. Aqaba is the only coastal city in Jordan and the largest and most populous city on the Gulf of Aqaba, located in the southernmost part of Jordan at the northeastern tip of the Red Sea between the continents of Asia and Africa, right across the Red Sea from Israel—and about a two-mile walk to the Israeli border.

This was 1974, and so this area of Jordan was very close to the occupied territories that the Israeli army so swiftly took from the Egyptians in the six-day war in June of 1967. Called "The Setback" by the Arabs, it was a stunning defeat on several fronts. It was the third Arab–Israeli war since Israel had declared independence in 1948, and as a result of it, Israel occupied the Sini Peninsula, the Gaza Strip, the Golan heights, and East Jerusalem. In just six days, Israel had doubled its size.

As Aqaba was in such proximity to the occupied territories, Jordan had not invested in updating the infrastructure just in case the Israelis one day seized it, too. As a result, the day that we were there, the water system in the whole town was not working. All the female members of our team had been dreaming of a hot shower in Aqaba to wash off the desert, so the next best option was to head off for a cleansing dip in the Gulf of Aqaba.

When we had been on camelback in the desert for two days and had not had the ability to clean ourselves, our Western noses were very happy to smell saltwater on our skin rather than what was there before. The beach was a wide sandy strip that went for what seemed forever in both directions. It was an extension of the valley we had just ridden through out into the gulf, and the shallow slope into the water gave tourists the chance to see the coral and fish of the gulf—by glass-bottom boat, snorkeling, or renting scuba equipment. The slope meant that even if members of our party had never scuba dived before, they could have the experience with very little risk of drowning. My mother and I were the only two adventurous souls who rented tanks and went for a dive.

It was the first time my mother had ever had a scuba experience (and the last in her life as well), while I had become a certified diver while attending my second trimester at Pepperdine in Malibu. So the dive master kept an eye on my mother more than on me, and we set off walking backward into the calm water.

The Red Sea is one of those great scuba places. The beach was very shallow, and we would never even get below one atmosphere, or 33 feet, so my mother was never going get in any trouble. And I was right by her side. As we glided peacefully under the surface, the fish were not spooked and would come close enough so that we could see their iridescent colors and the graceful turns and twists they performed by swimming in unison above the coral.

Sadly we were told that the coral was not as abundant as in years past, as it had been ripped up and taken as souvenirs by so many who came to the resort town for rest and relaxation.

At about the 40-minute mark, I got out of the water while the instructor was still with my mother under the water. There happened to be a girl on the trip a little older than me, so I sat on the beach talking to her. As my mother emerged (the scuba instructor not far away and having his eyes on her all the time), she was startled to see me sitting there chatting, as she had thought that she was surely leaving the water first. With a grin on her tired face after spending nearly an hour swimming inside a real-world aquarium, she said, "You abandoned me and came to talk to a young lady?" We laughed as we both could now say that we had scuba dived in the Red Sea. Put a check mark next to that one on our lifetime experience list. We were checking off a few boxes on this trip.

We went back to Beirut, and I was inspired by what I had seen and by my desire to take more photographs so I could capture the history that I was encountering up close. I had taken a photography class at Pepperdine, and Chris Albright, the head of Pepsi who was on the Camel Caravan trip, gave me the opportunity to try and shoot a commercial photograph of a Pepsi can that they could use in their print advertising.

I found out very quickly that I didn't have the skill set in commercial color photography to do exactly what they wanted, which was for the Pepsi can to sweat, with highlights on the droplets to give the viewer a sense of cool refreshment. This was before digitization when I could have just created the sweat on a computer, but here I needed to get the light and special effects just right, and it was beyond me and the equipment I possessed. So advertising photography was not in my immediate future.

Neither was Cheryl. Our relationship that year had been wonderful and full of joys and experiences that filled parts of my life that helped to bring me into manhood. Now that I was in Beirut, she wanted to cash in her life insurance and come to Beirut as well. I had made no promises, but now that I had gone on the Caravan trip and come back to Beirut, I realized that I did not want Cheryl to be there, and that realization made me also realize that she and I were not destined to be a couple long term, and our relationship was done. It wasn't a long emotional journey. It was just a change of scenery, and when I was more than 7,000 miles away from her, the distance did not make the heart grow fonder.

First love is not necessarily a lifetime commitment. And for me, I really was enamored more with the idea of the girl than with having a girlfriend that I was sleeping with. So when I left and went to Beirut, I was engaged by Beirut. I wasn't even missing Cheryl. And she called long distance, which was difficult to get through because, in my mind, I was thinking (and I'm exaggerating a bit), "Why are you bothering me? I'm over here. You're over there. We'll talk about it when I get back." Of course, when I would get back would be more than a year later, with my Year-in-Europe program coming up after this trip to Beirut.

However, she didn't want to let something go that she thought was pretty good. So I was speaking up for what I knew was right for me and told her on the phone that it was best if she did not join me in Beirut. She was upset, but I knew it was the best for us both. She got the message.

I had loved the Camel Caravan trip, but I was getting bored playing golf and squash and having no real friends in the city. And I had just broken up with my girlfriend. So my father spoke to a man in our building who worked for Price International to see if they could find work for his bored 18-year-old son. This guy called another guy, and soon I had a job offer: I would be leaving for Manama Bahrain to work on the docks and supervise the unloading of Price's construction materials off of transport ships. It would keep me busy for the last two months of the summer before going to Heidelberg. And it would put some additional spending money in my pocket.

It was so far beyond my imagined job field that I said yes, at once. After all, what could go wrong working on the docks in Bahrain in the steamy heat of June through August? I was about to find out, and painfully so.

7

A DANGEROUS JOB

Bahrain was hot. The temperature was more than 100 degrees Fahrenheit in late June 1974, and the humidity was 95 to 99% without a cloud in the sky to block the penetrating rays of the sun. It was so hot and humid that I would drink a gallon of water a day, and nothing would come out of me but sweat. I tried to move as little as possible and let the Bahraini guys do the work.

I was in Bahrain as an 18-year-old to work on the docks in Manama representing Price International, a company that was in oil service—installing concrete-coated steel pipes on the seabed to connect well heads offshore to storage and processing facilities onshore. Price imported the concrete and steel pipes, and at a Bahraini plant, they coated the pipes before they were taken out to sea and laid on the ocean bottom.

All of the materials came into the port via freighter, where they were loaded onto trucks and taken to the plant. The company wanted a trustworthy person to take inventory of the incoming material, to coordinate the stevedores, and to generally be the company's eyes on the docks. I was that guy.

So my job was to make sure that no pilferage was happening and that work happened in a reasonable period, as the company paid for the dock time when the ships were tied up. I wasn't supposed to do the manual labor, which probably made the burly Bahraini stevedores relieved. I was a skinny kid, still at about 105 pounds, and these stevedores work with their muscles all day, every day, for years. These guys were big, and they were strong. And I was this guy, half the size of most of them, telling them to work harder. And I would definitely be at a disadvantage if I did challenge anyone for stealing. So I had to keep an eye on everyone working and make sure all went on the up and up.

The only way I could do that, I realized, was to do some work as well, as I needed to get the respect of the stevedores. So when sacks of cement would come off the ships in a large sling that was lowered onto the dock, they had to be picked up and thrown onto a truck. I got in there with the stevedores and was throwing 40-pound bags of cement around like they were a tenth of that weight, and all of a sudden, after the disbelief wore off, the big Bahraini dockworkers were embarrassed by this little kid working harder than they were. So they started working harder, too.

I wouldn't throw cement bags for hours and hours. I would do it for 15 or 20 minutes at a time. But the desired impact had been created. Then I would drink a lot of water and never have to pee, ever.

I lived in Manama in a house owned by Price International, which was about a 10-minute drive from the dock. It had four or five bedrooms, and in each bedroom, there were two basic beds with sheets and blankets, but nobody used the blankets because it was too hot, even at night. I would shower, eat breakfast, work on the docks for 12 hours, come home, eat dinner, shower, and then sleep. That was my routine.

There was no art on the walls, nothing more than bare essentials. There was a TV in the living room, but the BBC was the only English-language channel, and its hours were limited. But no one in that house was there on vacation. The house was filled with grizzled oilfield workers, there for two months at a time, and they were English-speaking but not all from America. They came from Australia and Britain, and a couple of the older guys would sit up at night and have a whiskey and watch whatever was on TV. But not me. After a long hot day of work, I was fine just getting some sleep.

I didn't have much to do with the other people living in the house because of the punishing work schedule. And they were all at least 20 years older than me. All I wanted to do was to eat and sleep. The food was prepared and ready when we arrived back, but I never saw any cooks. I was just glad it was there.

It was hard work. Especially for a kid who was

underdeveloped like me. Yet all work and no play was not my style, so there were a couple of times that, on the rare day off, I went with one of the workers to the British officer's club, which was an expat club in Manama. It wasn't fancy, but they had a snooker table, so I played snooker. Other guys went there to drink and, I think, to forget the situation they were in or just out of habit, but I didn't drink. I just wasn't in the mood for it. Some of these guys thought a gin and tonic was refreshing in the heat; I craved ice water.

I did enjoy learning how to play snooker with the people who would want to play. I had been doing a work-study job in Malibu as the rec room supervisor in the late evenings. There were two pool tables there, and I had become fairly proficient on a pool table playing eight ball and straight pool, but snooker is a different story. The curved sides to the pockets, the smaller balls, and a larger playing surface took some getting used to. I didn't make friends or generate contacts or anything like that. I was on this job and didn't want to invest any emotional energy in a place I knew I would only be in for a couple months. I knew that I would be leaving Bahrain soon, at the end of August. I just didn't realize that I would be leaving even sooner.

When my day of reckoning arrived, I had been working on the docks for about four or five weeks. In truth, it was a sliver of a dock that could berth three ships on either side. This was the end of the era of cargo ships, with cranes on the ships to lift things out of the hold. Now there would be containers that would be lowered directly onto the trucks. Back then, the ship's crane would swing the cargo out over the dock and lower it onto the dock or sometimes directly onto trucks. That's what we were doing today.

We had a truck that was receiving pipes off a Norwegian freighter. We were unloading 40-foot lengths of steel pipe—each weighing over a ton. We would put four pipes on the lower level of the truck's bed and then stack three more on top of that. So these seven pipes per load created almost eight tons of pipe that the trucks would transport to the coating plant.

The crane operator would lower the pipes to between two and three feet above the truck bed. Workers would position the pipes so they would line up to the pipes on the truck. Then, once in position, the crane operator would lower the pipe the rest of the way on to the truck bed.

This day, I was up on the truck bed, positioning some of the pipes. They had already lowered three pipes onto the back of this truck. The pipes are up about 50 feet in the air when the crane raises them from the cargo bay, and then it moves the pipe to exactly where it needs to be lowered onto the truck.

Normally, the pipes are lowered to the height that they can be comfortably pushed into position, about three feet above the bed of the truck. Somebody then makes sure that the pipes are lined up to the right spot and signals the crane operator that all is good to go, and the crane operator lowers the pipes the rest of the way.

As these two pipes were coming down toward the truck bed, I saw that they were at an angle to where they were supposed to slot in, so they would not have gone onto the load smoothly. One end of the pipes needed to be pushed to line them up properly, so I stood on the truck bed with one foot to give me leverage on the pipe by pushing against it and my other foot in the space that the pipe was going to go into.

While I was getting ready, the crane operator believed he'd been signaled and started lowering the pipes. As he lowered the pipes onto the bed of the truck and into that spot where the pipe was to go, my foot was still in that spot. And as the pipe came down, I couldn't get my foot out fast enough. So the pipe rolled down my leg and onto the front of my foot and crushed it straight with the leg.

I was stuck in that position for no more than 30 seconds, my foot crushed between the pipes. The screams were loud enough for the crane operator to realize his error and reverse the lift, and he pulled back up. Whether they were my screams or those of others on the dock, I am not sure. One of the big stevedores came over to the truck, and he put one of his huge hands around my waist and lifted me up right off the truck bed. He took about four or five big steps and loaded me into the passenger side of a Toyota Corolla.

Somebody then popped into the driver's seat, started the car, and we were on the way to the "American Hospital" in

Bahrain.

The first "modern" hospital on the Arabian side of the gulf, the hospital was started by the Mason family of New York City and the Dutch Reformed Church of New Brunswick, New Jersey, on January 26th, 1903. The Masons provided the money, and the Dutch Reformed provided the staff. In 1962, it was renamed the American Mission Hospital upon its expansion by the Emir of Bahrain. Throughout the hospital's history, the majority of healthcare workers at the hospital came from Western countries and India—but very few came from the United States.

We arrived at the hospital parking lot, and the driver went in to get help. It seemed like he'd been gone five or even ten minutes, and I said to myself, "I can't wait any longer. I gotta get in." So I got out of the car and hopped on my good left leg into the emergency room, not realizing, of course, that if I'd ever touched my bad right foot to the ground, I would have fallen over in debilitating pain onto the searing asphalt. But I was still in shock.

As soon as I got inside, I was greeted with general confusion. Some aides started running around to find a gurney to lay me on.

As I was lying on the gurney, the nurse who put me there helped me remove my pants and the soft leather boots I was wearing. Amazingly, I was still in shock as the boot came off my foot, and there really was no pain, but then nothing was touching any part of my foot after it was freed from my boot.

A doctor came over to evaluate me. He was from India. He held up my leg by grabbing right above the top of my ankle on the injured foot. He looked at how the ankle was still in place at a right angle to the leg, but everything in front of the ankle was at a left angle and following the line of my leg. The boot had acted as a super-tough skin, keeping my own skin from bursting like the skin of a grape that is flattened, but everything inside the skin was crushed and broken.

It was hot and humid in the hospital, and the place reeked of sweat. That was affecting me more than my foot, initially. The doctor was in his late 20s, and for all I knew, this was his first professional gig, a job in Manama to get some hands-on experience, which he was certainly about to get. He mirrored the lack of cleanliness in Bahrain, as well as the tradition of not wearing deodorant, which allowed his fragrance to get to my senses before he was close enough for me to focus on him. He looked at the foot from the end of the gurney and put his hand with untrimmed nails that had received little grooming attention in quite some time around the crushed and broken bottom half of my foot, and in one motion, he moved it up to be in line with my ankle. As he was doing it, I will never forget the words he said in his heavy Indian-accented English: "Oh, this is not right, it should be more like this." And it was on the word "this" that he moved the bottom half of my foot into alignment with the ankle, and the pain took over from the shock. I remember they started wrapping the foot in a cast, but I mercifully faded to black.

When I awoke, I was in a hospital bed with bright sunlight coming through the window of a private room. I was also in a fog. As my fuzzy vision began to focus, I looked down at my slightly elevated foot and thought it was moving. I did not have the benefit of my glasses, without which my vision was poor at best. I noticed my glasses were on the nightstand next to the bed and twisted to reach for them so I could see.

As I put the glasses on and blinked to focus more clearly, I was greeted by a line of large black ants that ran from the floor, up the leg of the bed, across the sheets, up the cast, and into the end of my open-toed cast, where dinner was served. I tried to shake them off.

I know that nerve receptors can transmit pain signals as fast as 390 feet a second, but reality slowed it all down. My brain knew that pain was going to hit from me shaking my foot to free it of the dining ants, and in slow motion, the wave of pain traveled up my leg, up the right side of my body, and up my neck to explode in my brain. It was a blinding flash of light that emptied my brain of anything but appreciation that I would embrace the blackness of shock once again.

There is a story that I learned about an ant in a book *Folktales of the Arabian Peninsula*. Suleiman I, commonly known as Suleiman the Magnificent in the West and Suleiman the Lawgiver in the Islamic world, was Sultan of the Ottoman Empire from 1520 until his death in 1566, and his caliphate ruled over at least 25 million people. Among his many talents, it is said he had the ability to understand and speak with animals.

One day, he saw an ant and spoke with it and asked how much food it ate during a year. The ant replied that it ate three grains of rice in a year. So, Suleiman put the ant in a box with three grains of rice.

After one year, he looked in the box and saw that only one and a half grains of rice had been eaten. He asked the ant why this was.

The ant replied, "When I am outside, God provides. Now that I am in a box, I did not know if you would forget me. I want to live, so I have eaten less food than I normally would."

I think that the entire population of ants within traveling distance of my damaged foot believed that God was providing for them in that hospital room, a place that was as much a prison to me as it was an infirmary.

Confined to a room, in a bed that I was unable to move out of while waiting for my exit visa to be processed to get back to Beirut and the American University Hospital, I engaged in a constant battle using the end of a crutch to combat the ants as they traveled across the floor—a battle that lasted for one week.

When a foreign worker enters the Kingdom of Bahrain, they surrender their passport to the government, which holds it until the foreigner exits the country. It's kind of an insurance policy against foreigners committing any offenses against the state and trying to flee. At the appointed departure time on your visa, if the state doesn't need to detain you for any reason, you are given your passport as you exit the country. Due to my accident, I was a little over a month away from leaving the country, so my passport had to be located and the visa updated to allow for my early departure. And there were logistics to arrange to get a flight back to Beirut.

I can only imagine what the mood in Beirut was like when someone from Price International called my parents to tell them that I had been in an accident on the docks in Manama. Sketchy details and an unknown prognosis for your son certainly create the dread that all parents feel when the phone rings and they learn that their child is injured and in a hospital in some far-off place with very little support. I can only imagine my mother's fear rekindling in her brain about the health of her son. From youthful surgeries to broken bones learning to skateboard when I was 10 to now an industrial accident. What next?

My father worked with the Price International people, the American embassy, and other contacts that he had to get on a plane to Bahrain. It took seven days to process me out of the country, and then my father picked me up at the hospital and took me to the airport. He got me on the plane for the ride back to Beirut. He even arranged for a first-class ticket so that I would have extra legroom. It's almost a six-hour flight from Bahrain to Beirut, and once back in Lebanon, my father took me straight to the hospital.

Upon checking in to the American University Hospital in Beirut, a higher class of medical professional started to get to work in a sterile teaching hospital with Western-educated and board-certified staff. Not unsurprisingly, the foot had become infected in that hazy week of confinement combined with the constant battle with ants as I fought off waves upon waves of them heading to the promised land of feasting on an open wound. The pressure of the swelling inside my cast should have been a clue as to how bad my foot had become, but no one in Bahrain was taking any notice.

My foot had become so infected that it was very close to being at the point where they would have to amputate. The doctors were frank with me. They said, "You know, if we see streaks of blood coming up your leg or infection coming up your leg, that means this infection is getting into your bloodstream, meaning we haven't cured the infection, and it's gotten gangrene; at that point we will have to amputate to save your life." It was swollen and puss-filled, and the idea of losing my foot was making the ever-present pain begin to throb.

But the doctors helped ease my worry by saying, "Here's our plan to make sure that we don't have to. We're going to give you all sorts of antibiotics. We're going to keep your foot elevated. We're going to clean it on a regular basis. We're going to help." They were not American doctors, but they were organized and well trained, and I felt much better about being on the receiving end of their plan than I had felt about anything in that hospital in Bahrain. They had a plan!

They hit me with every kind of antibiotic in massive doses, and they got the infection down and saved my foot. They cured the smelly infection that was just a small sliver of a step away from being gangrene. I was relieved, but I was far from done.

After they tamed the infection, they operated on my foot to try to attempt to correct the stupidity of the Indian doctor who bent my foot back into shape and nearly destroyed it. The surgeons in Beirut would try to make this blob of bones into a semblance of a foot. So they had to re-break many of the bones in my foot to set it as right as they could.

Since we had private insurance and the bills were being paid by Price International, we probably got the best treatment. The surgeons rebuilt my foot as much as they could and put it in a cast. Now I had to learn to walk all over again, so I had to learn how to use crutches first just so I could go to the bathroom.

And then, two weeks before I had to leave for my year abroad in Heidelberg, they put me in a walking cast, which was plaster of Paris, up to my knee. And then on the bottom of the cast was a two- or three-inch square piece of rubber that they insert into the plaster of Paris underneath your foot. This piece was more to the heel than to the center of the foot because the center of my foot was not a stable place to put anything.

The Price International people were really very good to me. I'm sure they were afraid of some kind of legal action against them, but that's not the way I was brought up. There are risks that you assume when you take on any job. I encountered those risks, and it was not the company's fault. I believe they paid for all the hospital bills, and that's why I had a private room. They also paid me as if I was working on the docks of Bahrain for that month. I was making $900 a month working on the docks, so I got another $900 for being in the hospital for a month.

There was little to do while in a hospital bed, save eating the cookies that my mother's friend Katie Patterson, whose husband Stan worked with my dad, brought me every day. I think she was trying to fatten me up while I was captive to her baking skills—which were awesome! So, I began to deal with my boredom by reading some of the paperback books that visitors left for me. My mom collected books from her friends who had current English books that they were reading that they all probably had bought for airplane rides. Back in that day, the only entertainment on an airplane was to read. So you would buy a book at the airport and read it on the plane. And then everybody became a lending library after that.

I never had been a reader for pleasure in my life up to that point. Indeed, I had avoided reading in my studies, and maybe that's why I had just passed such an average academic year at Pepperdine.

In that hospital room, with time ticking ever so slowly like a dripping faucet that one drop at a time tries to fill a bathtub, I came to find that engrossing myself in a story turned the daily drip of time into a richly flowing stream, and my days passed much more pleasantly and quickly.

I found a release in allowing my imagination to become part of an author's weaving a story through words on paper. In that month, I learned to read for pleasure. I would suffer pains in my foot and troubles with my right knee later in life from my altered gait, but in exchange for that pain, the pleasure of the literary world opened up for me. I would call that more than a fair exchange.

As September began, I was saying goodbye to Beirut. I was heading to my Year-in-Europe program with Pepperdine University in Heidelberg, Germany, with a walking cast on my foot. It was a good thing I could walk, as my friend Stu was to meet me in London. We had decided to poke around London for a few days before we headed to Germany, as Stu had never been to London. In fact, Stu had never been outside the United States. The great thing about youth is that you don't let things stop you. So Stu was going to get his London tour guide in the end, a little slowed down but still standing. The ants had not gotten me yet.

8

WHEN A MAN IS TIRED
OF LONDON . . .

In September of 1974, I was on my way to Heidelberg, Germany, for my fall semester in their Year-in-Europe program. And my first stop was London, where I flew with my parents, as my father had business at the Farnborough Air Show. Within the space of a month, I had traveled from a fetid, ant-infested hospital room in Bahrain to a plush hotel suite at the Inn on the Park hotel in London.

It was across the street from the Ambassador Club, which is a private club seen in the first Bond film, *Dr. No*. Bond plays chemin de fer in the casino, and viewers can see Hyde Park from inside the club. My dad was a member for business purposes, so my parents and I had dinner there. It was a very upscale place where you needed to wear a tie if you were a guy. My father did not give me any gambling money for the casino this time. I think we all had learned his lesson; besides, the table stakes here were much higher than they were in Lebanon. It was much like the ambiance of the casino in Monaco—being there and experiencing the buzz of excitement of high-stakes gaming is enough without having to pay for the entertainment.

It was at this hotel that I met up with my friend Stu, who was also heading to Heidelberg and whom I had convinced to meet up with me in London. I was sitting in the lobby of the Inn on the Park Hotel, eating strawberries and cream and generally enjoying English civilization, when Stu rolled in, looking like he'd been on the wrong end of a long trip. He had been fortunate to get a ride into central London from the lady who sat next to him on the flight; otherwise, he was totally lost! He's a big, solid guy, but his face, when he saw me sitting there in my English glory, looked like he wanted to smack me or laugh at me. He did the latter.

Turns out that the airlines lost Stu's luggage, so we hatched a plan to turn this to his advantage. As I hobbled on my walking cast, we went to the airline ticket offices to see what they could do for Stu. The airline offered him some funds to go buy some new clothes. Well, we got him more than a new toothbrush. We got him a nice new outfit to wander around London in. And the airline paid for that. We thought that was a great deal. We looked at each other with that high jinks kind of gleam, as we knew that this was a plan that could work again.

I checked out of my parents' hotel because it was too posh for the likes of Stu and me; we were now on our student budget. So we found ourselves a place just off Piccadilly

Circus. It was the same hotel that we had stayed in as a family in 1968 when we made our grand tour on $5 a day. Our room was to the left of the big Coca-Cola sign that faces the Circus, and that's why we got a good price.

London Piccadilly Circus 1974

I loved being in London, even in my hobbled state. I had been here before when I was a 13-year-old and had returned again on my stopovers to Beirut once or twice, staying for a day or so. I would go into London to explore rather than staying in the transit lounge for up to 20 hours until my flight to Beirut was ready to go. Now I was here after a pretty adventurous time in the Middle East, and the thing that struck me most was the organized society that I found in London.

There were crowds—London is much bigger than Beirut—but they were organized and polite crowds. There was an orderly, civilized vibe to the city that I really admired. My nose was happier, too. In the Middle East, you become so inured to the rather Baroque collection of smells—human, animal, mysterious—that you don't notice them after a while. But when they are not swirling around you, you notice the absence. So London, even though it's not the cleanest city in the world, smelled clean to me. Drivers even stopped for pedestrians at zebra crossings (which we call crosswalks). It was a concept so foreign to the Middle East that it made London far more exotic in a way. But I didn't feel like a tourist in London. It felt familiar.

Which, of course, was a bonus for Stu, as he was pretty much at sea for the beginning of our trip. The first night in our Piccadilly Circus hotel, Stu told me, "I know I'd have to get over jet lag. Wake me up in the morning. Do whatever you have to do."

So that first morning together, I was up and dressed and ready to go explore London. And Stu was still sleeping. I tried to wake him up, but nothing worked. So, recalling his order to do whatever it took to get him conscious and moving, I got a glass of water, and I poured it on him.

It certainly woke him up, and he was conscious and moving. In fact, he started chasing me. So I was hobbling down the hallway outside the room, and then he emerged from the room to chase after me, and then he stopped on a dime as he realized that he was completely naked. So he hightailed it back into the room. We had a laugh over that, and then we hit the streets of the city of which Samuel Johnson famously said, "When a man is tired of London, he is tired of life."

I was now off crutches and just walking around with this big club of a walking cast, which gave me a monster limp because the piece of rubber underneath it made my right leg a couple of inches higher than my left leg. I had planned the routes we were going to take and what we were going to do. It wasn't like I was superior or a tour guide. I was excited to share my experience of London with my friend, who was making his first visit to the great city. We were two buddies going along, and he just sort of went along with the flow of being in a big city. We were still equals in everything.

Except maybe pub speak. Our favorite pub was right off of Piccadilly Circus, and Stu was amazed that we could order beer in a pub, which was legal because we were 18 years old and that's the drinking age in Britain. This was a Courage pub, and that was fine, as I preferred John Courage beer to Watney's. The pubs in Britain are known by the main beer they serve, or used to be, until breweries consolidated and international distilleries started buying them up.

There's a different feel to the whole concept of alcohol in England. It seemed much more relaxed, and as a result, people didn't abuse it. Well, of course they did, as they do everywhere, but to two 18-year-olds, the fact that we could have it when we wanted it made us want it less. Stu's eyes popped when I ordered faggots and mash. No, I wasn't using a very offensive word to ask for some gay guys to come to the bar. Faggots, in British cuisine, are pork meatballs, and they are delicious. The meatballs' name comes from an old British term for a bundle of sticks and refers to the way the meatballs are shaped and wrapped in fat before baking them. Mash is short for mashed potatoes, and Stu soon got the hang of ordering pub food. He needed his energy, as we crammed a lot of London into five days.

We went to the Tower of London and saw the ancient castle on the hill, the Beefeater guards, and that moat that had so impressed me when I was 13 as I thought about King Arthur and medieval times. Now I had much more history inside my head and knew that there were scholarly debates about whether Arthur was a man or a myth, but it still thrilled me to be back in front of the Tower. We also enjoyed the classic London street performer working the street in front of it who could bend a metal bar with his bare hands. His talents could have been used by many guests of the Tower in days of yore. He was a great showman and had 50 to 60 people around him as he was doing his act, working for the generosity of the tips they threw into the hat that he passed at the end of the routine.

We would always stop for street performers, as we didn't just rush from place to place. We saw the changing of the guard at Buckingham Palace. And even with my walking cast, I walked from Westminster, past St. James, to Buckingham Palace, which isn't that far, but it's still a bit of a hike. I refused to be slowed down at all by the walking cast. Of course, the Underground in London is great for getting to all the places you want to go. Stu had never been on a subway, let alone on one of the most iconic in the world. The Underground, which had become the bomb shelter for London during World War II and saved countless lives, took us from one side of London to the other.

When you're guiding a friend through a city that you've already been to and which they have not, you see things again freshly, as if for your first time. So in some respects, I remembered more about seeing the Tower of London with Stu than I did when I saw it at age 13. I remember that street performer outside the Tower of London that I saw with Stu as if we were there yesterday.

We went to the antique market at Spitalfields in the East End of London on the Tube, alighting at Liverpool Street and making the 10-minute trek to a sensory overload, with antiques and clothes and records and food, and people everywhere. We went to Christopher Wren's architectural marvel, St. Paul's Cathedral, where the Whispering Gallery fascinated me the way all those Crusader castles and ancient ruins in Athens and Rome had done. How did these architects conjure such wonders?

It turns out that Wren never meant to create such an acoustic marvel, which sits 90 feet above the crossing of the nave. It's a circular walkway that looks down on the nave below, and it became a popular meeting spot after the consecration of St. Paul's in 1708. People soon discovered that if you whisper along the curving wall, then anyone standing anywhere along that same wall will be able to hear you. It's a quirk that Wren didn't design, but again, that's the beauty of history. What we think we know is often different from what actually happened. I love finding the connection between the two.

We kept going on our London tour and enjoyed the shops and food at Covent Garden and the speakers at Marble Arch offering their opinions to the world from the top of their apple crates. They made their impassioned pleas about whatever subject they were talking about, so when Stu and I walked past and there wasn't anybody there, we both got up on the apple crate. I think I said, "Friends, Romans, countrymen . . ." or something like that. I used a loud, theatrical voice that was appropriate for Speaker's Corner. I had an audience of one, Stu.

We went to Simpson's in the Strand for a traditional British lunch. The restaurant had begun in 1828 as a chess club and then grew into a famous destination for roast beef and Yorkshire pudding. We dined like kings, and then afterward, we went to see *The Mousetrap*. I am pretty sure that this was Stu's first time in a theater, and that was especially nice because, as I have mentioned, I love *The Mousetrap*, and he did, too. It is kind of a tradition for me to go and see this play—the longest continuously running play in history—when I am there with people visiting for the first time.

We took the hovercraft up to Greenwich to see the observatory and the Prime Meridian. And we also went to see *The Student Prince*, a four-act operetta that was playing in London and a perfect prelude to our imminent residence as students in Heidelberg.

The Student Prince is a show that epitomizes pure romance. The prince, Karl Franz, is sent to university at Heidelberg to finish his studies. And he knows that he would be accepted into the aristocratic society and fraternity there. But he disguises himself and uses his disguise as a "commoner" to mingle with the common fraternity. And, of course, he falls in love with Kathie, the daughter of the innkeeper at the inn where the prince likes to sink a few pints of beer. I loved this juxtaposition of the prince who enjoys common life and falls in love with a commoner, but of course, the prince has been promised in marriage to a princess since childhood, and it looks like true love is doomed.

And it is, with the prince marrying the princess but still knowing in his heart that Kathie is his true love.

The Student Prince resonated with me as I prepared to go to Heidelberg. I was in no way an aristocrat, but I did wonder if I would fit in and, more so, if I, too, would find true love. It was the sense of possibility and the romance that spoke, or rather sang, to me, and I was excited to be heading off to a place that now was the most romantic place

I could envision going.

Then there was a full day spent joining my parents at the Farnborough Air show. Not normally on a tourist agenda of London, but with my dad spending the week at the show conducting business, we had the opportunity and took it. You hear about some of the marvels of technology, but nothing replaces seeing and experiencing it firsthand.

The idea that a machine of heavy steel can actually fly is astounding enough, but to see the Hawker Siddeley Harrier Jump Jet actually swoop in, stop in midair, and then land is pretty astounding. Then moments later, it took off vertically, with the nose rising and the turbo jets kicking in and sending the plane straight up into the clouds like a rocket.

Stu and I were then treated to a test flight aboard Lockheed's commercial entrant into the wide-bodied passenger jet market, the L1011. My father was the lead salesperson for Lockheed in the Middle East and would later sell some of the jets to both Gulf Air and Saudia Airlines. But the highlight of the airshow was also provided by Lockheed that year.

Major James Sullivan and Major Noel Widdifield had set a new world speed record from New York to London at just over 1,807 miles per hour—less than two hours—in the SR71 Blackbird! The Blackbird was Lockheed's long-range, high-altitude, Mach 3+ strategic reconnaissance aircraft. We were told that once the record was set in London, it took the plane as far as Amsterdam before the pilots could complete the turn back to England! And there it was on the tarmac, a sleek, black, missile-shaped twin-engine jet, for all to see and marvel at.

The five days in London flew by, and we were due in Heidelberg soon. My parents were still in London, and for the first time in my college career, we had a proper send-off, with both my mother and father there to say goodbye to me as I began my next adventure. That had never happened quite like this before. To be sure, they had said farewell when I left Beirut for Pepperdine, but this time it seemed more traditional, more like a proper parting. Maybe that's because we were all away from home, and so that idea of leaving home was more of a presence in my departure. At this point in my life, I had lived in several places, and while California was "home" in the sense that I had been born there and, but for three years in Hong Kong, had grown up there, I was increasingly seeing myself as a citizen of the world. An American, of course, but one who had the freedom and the desire to live abroad for a while. At that farewell with my parents in London, I just did not know how long "a while" would be.

And Stu and I had one more thing to do in London, that thing inspired by Stu's lost luggage at the beginning of our London trip. We had both seen the film *The Sting*, which had come out the year before in 1973. It's a wonderfully clever and entertaining tale, with that great Scott Joplin ragtime soundtrack, about an elaborate con pulled off by

Paul Newman and Robert Redford to get revenge for their murdered friend. We had no such lofty purpose, but we remembered how we had benefited from the airlines and the lost luggage at the beginning of our London adventure, so we fancied that we could do the same again to the airlines. We even flicked a finger off our noses, the way they did in *The Sting* to signal to their co-conspirators that the game was afoot.

I had an extra suitcase that had decals on it and looked well-used. So we put a couple of T-shirts in it and figured out a way to have it get "lost in transit" because that loss might get us some cash to buy some new clothes.

We had to take a plane to Frankfurt. So we used the check-in for the airline in Central London. As Stu spoke to the ticket agent and checked in all our bags, as he was playing sherpa to me given my hobbled state, I reached across the counter and got a baggage tag. We got our tickets to Frankfurt, and we put the tag on the old suitcase with the T-shirts inside and put it on the luggage conveyor belt. It never got noticed by the agent that while we were going to Frankfurt, that old suitcase was going to Pittsburgh.

And, you know, that was fun, but we didn't take advantage of the airlines, and we never tried to put a claim in at the end. But we succeeded in our "sting," as I got that suitcase to go to Pittsburgh. Lo and behold, they found it and got it back to us in Heidelberg. But just knowing the ropes enough to know how to do it showed my familiarity with travel. I knew we had a better chance of success by checking in at the central London kiosk, versus going to the airport to check in. I had figured out how to get our substitute luggage tag and put it on the bag and then get the bag on its way without being noticed. You know, had things turned out differently, I could have been a great terrorist.

Of course, I am kidding, as I have no desire to harm anyone for any reason. My point is that it's always surprising to me to see what people do or do not notice in their environment. I was awakening to the world rapidly after nearly losing my foot in Bahrain. The fact that I had started reading now helped focus my vision, as storytellers need detail to make their stories come to life. Looking back on it now, I realize how much I didn't know. But I remember that at that time, I felt that I knew enough to succeed at whatever I was going to do next, and "next" was going to happen in Germany.

As Stu and I flew to Frankfurt to begin our Year-in-Europe, I thought about all that I had accomplished and what I wanted to do going forward. I had managed to get through my first year at Pepperdine and even made the dean's list once upon a time. I had made friends, and my best one was sitting next to me on the plane. I got to spend time with my parents in Beirut and to travel the Middle East with my mother on the back of a camel. I had experienced my first love with Cheryl and my first breakup with her as well. Or, as I had said, I thought it was first love until I met the woman who really would be that person, and even then, she wasn't. I know it sounds complicated, but we will come to that.

As we landed in Germany, I felt confident that I had grown as a person, and my experience of living and traveling abroad had set me up for my time to come in Heidelberg. I also felt that my friendship with Stu was one of the most important things in my life. I had never had a "best" friend like him, and I felt completely confident that he would "have my back," as I would have his.

Stu came from a tough childhood, with a single mother and not a lot of excess capital to create the good life. I was going to share with him, as I had in London, what life could be like. Not as some kind of superior being, but as his friend. For the first time in my life, I had a real, true friend. And I knew it. It was a life milestone for me.

When we landed in Frankfurt, we had to take a train to Heidelberg, which is a bit more than an hour to the south by the express. The train station straddles the old, medieval Heidelberg and the new city, and I felt like I was traveling back in time, just like I did in Beirut, though not nearly as far back in time!

While a lot of Germany had been destroyed during World War II about three decades earlier, Heidelberg had escaped the bombs because it was not an industrial center, nor was it a hub of German army transportation. The most damage came from the German army itself when it blew up three arches of the old bridge, which opened in 1788 and connects the old city across the Neckar River. I instantly loved the old city, with its cobblestone streets and its Baroque and Renaissance architecture mixed up with the older styles. And we were in awe of the magnificent red-sandstone ruins of Heidelberg Castle, a noted example of melding those various architectural styles around a main building of Renaissance architecture, which stands on Königstuhl Hill.

Hills were going to be a part of life in Heidelberg, much to the chagrin of the guy still in the walking cast. Our residence in the city, the Moore Haus, was also on a hill, roughly at the same level as the castle, which was very close to it. We had to walk up hundreds of steps to reach the house, which was owned by Pepperdine and which made Pepperdine unique in the year abroad programs at the time because they owned the building as opposed to leasing someone else's building.

It was a little bastion of America on the hill, and now that Stu and I were here, it was going to become an even more interesting place. I was determined to live to the fullest in Heidelberg, walking cast or not. I knew how lucky I had been to be accepted into this program as a sophomore when it was the province mainly of juniors and seniors. I had taken up one of those spaces, and I was determined to prove that Pepperdine, once again, had made the right decision in choosing me. Stu and I were Americans abroad, and we were going to have the best year of our lives.

9

HEIDELBERG

I n 1963, Pepperdine University began its "Year-in-Europe" program in Heidelberg, West Germany, and in 1965, it bought a permanent facility located just 300 yards from Heidelberg Castle. The Moore Haus was a spacious four-story mansion that looked like a little castle itself, built in the German country villa style that features stone arches and leaded glass windows and sloping roofs framed with timber, with wooden infill vertically decorating the frames. All sitting majestically on a hill.

Because of its location, Moore Haus is one of the highest houses on the castle hill and is visible from the famous Philosopher's Way and Old Town Heidelberg. Everyone who goes to Heidelberg Castle passes by Moore Haus. You can't miss it.

The house was built in 1906 by an academic and had quite a history itself. After World War I, the Schmitthelm family, who became rich by manufacturing down comforters, bought it. During World War II, the mansion housed people who had been bombed out of Mannheim, about 12 miles northwest. After the war, the US Army turned the house into the headquarters for the CIC, the forerunner of CIA, and used it to interrogate former Nazis. In 1953, West Germany returned the place to the Schmitthelm family, but they were comfortable in their new house, so once again, it became a military base, this time for the new German Federal Army.

Pepperdine bought it in 1965 for $100,000, the same amount it had cost to build it in 1906 (it is worth well over $1 million today), and a year later, students moved into the newly renovated dorm house, named after J.C. Moore Jr., a Pepperdine controller who had championed the Year-in-Europe program.

Heidelberg – Moore Haus in winter of 1974

The basement (or lower floor, as it did have a door to the outside on the front of the house) housed the breakfast room, an office, the laundry, and a utilities room. Each morning, we would trek down to the basement to have bread with jam or cheese and coffee before we began our studies.

When you entered after the climb up flights of stairs from the street, you landed on the first floor, which housed the reception area, the library, and the apartment for Frau Ronsohoff and her mother, who looked after us.

On the second floor, which was accessible from a stairway off the reception area on the first, was where the female students lived. And we were on the third floor, which you reached from a separate stairway located outside. It housed the men, and there was no direct connection between it and the second floor, and it had a wonderful view over Old Heidelberg and the Neckar Valley.

Frau Ronsohoff looked after the 36 students who lived in the house. Frau Ronsohoff was in her 50s, and her mother was in her 70s, and they were good to us, but they also kept a proper distance so that we knew they were the adults in the house, so to speak. Frau Ronsohoff also taught German to us. As both a teacher and a house mother with an apartment, she had enough compensation to make it worth her while. At Moore Haus, there was a garage carved into a rock cave that barely fit Herr Doktor Luft's Mercedes Benz.

Herr Doktor Luft was the head of the Pepperdine program in Germany. He was a German historian in his late 30s and a touch aloof, conscious of his title. And you had to be conscious of it as well, and pretty much all titles in

Germany, which had its own strict formalities. Dr. Luft lived in a little town about a half hour's drive from Heidelberg, in a historic house dating from the Middle Ages that was a heritage house, and it was charming. I got to see it when I went there for dinner later in the year.

There were visiting professors each semester from Pepperdine in Malibu who would come over and, according to their area of expertise, teach us upper-level classes in their disciplines. One of the semesters, Dr. Steven Lemley came over, and he taught some of the religion classes and a philosophy class. He was also a Christian pastor, and so he brought that conservative Christian sensibility to Heidelberg. Each semester saw a new visiting professor arrive, as Heidelberg was kind of a sabbatical for them. They did not live at Moore Haus but in an apartment on the other side of the Neckar River.

Heidelberg – Houses along the Nekar 1974

We'd have classes from the visiting professor as well as from Herr Doktor Luft, who taught history and philosophy. Frau Ronsohoff, our housemother, taught me beginning German. I did not have any German language knowledge whatsoever before I went to Heidelberg, but now that I was there, it was a requirement to take a German class at whatever level you were at. So it was beginning German for me as well as over half the students there.

I was never good in English or in German. I never really got the structure of sentences and the finer points of grammar and so on; I just knew how to speak English. And I couldn't translate speaking English to speaking German. The Germans construct their sentences differently, and they'll put the verb at the end, which mangled any kind of direct translation.

"*Möchten Sie mit mir ausgehn,*" is one of the few phrases I can remember because that's what you'd say to a girl. Would you like to go out with me? "Hey, *was möchtest du machen?*" Hey, what would you like to do? So I learned more on the street in Heidelberg than in class. I would learn more phrases and words on the street, but I was a B to C student in my beginning German class because of sentence structure, tenses, and things like that, which made comprehension difficult. Even so, I could get by when we went out into town. I had learned on my travels that words are not the only way to communicate with someone, and gestures and expressions can be just as effective, along with a smile and laughter.

Things were quite lively on the romantic front in Heidelberg during that first semester. Stu was communicating with a girl that he'd left behind in California, and he was trying to be as loyal as he could to her while at the same time noticing all the attractive young women around him in Heidelberg. Little did he know that his California girlfriend pretty much cheated on him right after he left to join me in London.

To complicate matters, Sue, a fellow student, was starting to pay obvious attention to Stu, which was causing him difficulty because he was still attempting his loyalty mission to the disloyal young woman in California. Stu came to me and asked me if I could cozy up to Sue and distract her a little bit, not by trying to be boyfriend or anything, but just to take her gaze off him.

Heidelberg – Stu, Sue and Blake 1975

We started all hanging together as three, and then Sue and I would do things together when Stu was "busy." So, being the loyal friend, I did as he asked, and Sue and I started hanging together. Before too long, Sue became my girlfriend. Stu, on the other hand, remained pretty loyal to his girlfriend back home and would communicate with her through letters. Once a month—because phone calls were very expensive—they would have a brief phone call. And so his girlfriend kept this fiction going that they were still monogamous, but in truth, she was dating other people. Stu eventually figured it out, but by then, Sue and I were a team.

Sue was more Christian than I was by a long shot, and she was studying theology. And she was not as liberal as I was. She was a virgin when she got to Heidelberg, and I had thought she still was in that same state when we took a weekend trip to London together. We became intimate in London, and that's when she confessed that two weeks before, she had been intimate for the first time, but not with me. It has always been part of my nature to be very forgiving of that kind of thing, so it didn't harm our relationship, which continued until Sue left Heidelberg at the end of our second semester, and I left after the third.

And when I came back to the United States and thought that there was a chance we were going to be a couple when I returned home, I discovered that she was already dating someone else. I was her European romance. And much of that experience was so much better for having a romantic interest when seeing places and experiencing things. Sharing travel is far better than going alone. Sue will always have a fond place in my heart for the joys we shared there. I believed I was always looking for a long-term relationship, even though later in life, I'd have trouble taking it from a long-term relationship to a long-term commitment. But that wasn't an issue in Heidelberg.

During that first semester, I loved to just explore the city—and, indeed, I loved to explore Europe. I got to see Heidelberg just by going to class, which was held in the Amerika Haus, a cultural building in central Heidelberg. There was in a series of American houses created in Germany and Austria as a post-war plan to let German and Austrian citizens learn more about American culture and politics.

Amerika Haus was about a 15-minute hike down the hill and a bit longer going back up, and when my walking cast came off toward the end of the first semester, I had to learn to walk all over again without one leg higher than the other. That walk to and from Amerika Haus was my walking tutor.

Our classes were spread over roughly three and a half days each week, and while that might seem like a pretty lax schedule, it was on purpose. And those days were very full academic days. Pepperdine quite wisely wanted its students to have long weekends to be able to just hop on a train and visit Europe on our long weekends.

Haut-Koenigsbourg 1974

So, after classes on Thursday, we would sign out and tell our minders roughly where we were heading, then leave Amerika Haus and make the 20-minute walk to the train station. And then, with our Eurail passes in hand, we would then hop on the next train that came through. It didn't matter where it was going, as any destination was good for us, no matter what we had written in the sign-out book at Moore Haus.

Lindau – light house on Lake Constance 1975

Sometimes, after a busy week, we'd fall asleep on the train, and when we woke up, we'd get off at whatever the next stop was and explore that city. It was a very free and exciting way to travel. We went to France and to Holland and all over Germany. We made it up as we went.

Chenenseau France 1975

We were also traveling in student style, so we would have some salami, some cheese, some bread, and some wine or beer in our backpacks, and that's what we would eat over the weekend. We wouldn't spend our money at restaurants, but we might go to pubs to have some beers. We'd sometimes visit a few small towns during the course of a weekend, and then we would get back by Sunday night to check in and be

Amboise France – Chaple 1975

ready for classes Monday morning.

Sue and I went to London, and we didn't arrive back until later afternoon Monday, which was not allowed. Frau

Ronsohoff heard us come into the Moore Haus, but she never said anything to us, so we got away with it. Or so we thought.

London was not easy to get to, even by train. It was a long train trip to London and a long one coming back. It was not a trip you could do by departing on a Thursday afternoon and returning on a Sunday night if you wanted to have any quality time in London. We knew going out that we wouldn't be able to get permission to cut classes on Monday. So Sue and I decided that we'd have a nice couples weekend in London and miss classes on Monday. And we'd deal with the outcome rather than letting everybody in the world know that we were going to take an extra day on the road.

That same weekend, there was a train strike in the south of France. And the ripple effect of the strike disrupted numerous train schedules. And so, despite our plans to come back late, now we were going to be a lot later because we couldn't get back due to the train strike. Back in Heidelberg, Frau Ronsohoff and the administration were worried about where we were, and of course, we had not called to say we were going to be late.

So, we arrived back later, and Pepperdine gave me another letter of reprimand. Sue did not get one because I stepped up and took responsibility for it. The letter said, "You broke the rules, and we're not going to tolerate this again. If you're late coming back from a trip and we don't know about it, then, it's going to be far more severe than just a letter in your file." It seemed I was not immune to receiving letters of reprimand in Europe. I was a bicultural offender. But I took it seriously, as I was loving my life so far in Heidelberg, and the last thing I wanted to do was to get expelled from Germany!

The other great thing about the ease of travel in Europe was that I connected directly to my studies. When we were studying Charlemagne, I went to Aachen, which was where he had his throne. The city is about 175 miles northwest of Heidelberg, close to Cologne. It had been pretty heavily bombed during WWII, but the Palatine Chapel, which Charlemagne began at the end of the eighth century and where he was buried in 814, was still standing. And as I saw these places in my history books in person, history became even more alive to me. Now it wasn't a tour guide filling me on what great event had happened where I was now standing or what great building lay before me. I was doing it for myself with what I had learned from my history books and classes. And frankly with more depth of knowledge than the average tour guide.

Rotenburg 1975

Each semester, we also took historically important trips as a group. We were led by Herr Doktor Luft, and in our first semester, we traveled to Bavaria to see Mad King Ludwig's world in and around Munich. He was king of Bavaria from 1864 until his death in 1886. When Germany unified in 1871, Ludwig grew more remote from political life and pursued the projects that earned him his nickname, such as the construction of lavish palaces, including the fairy tale castle Neuschwanstein (it was the inspiration for Disneyland's Sleeping Beauty Castle) that he created as a retreat for the composer Richard Wagner, whose operas Ludwig loved.

Neuschwanstein 1975

We also went to Dachau, the Nazi concentration camp. But Herr Doktor Luft had taught us about Hitler and the Beer Hall Putsch and the Nazi regime. While we were touring the death camp, he didn't go into details, but he did address it. This really did happen. He wasn't a denier or anything like that. And he let Dachau speak for itself, the way historical places can.

Dachau itself was stark. And if your imagination ran even just a little bit, you could easily see how awful it would have been to have been imprisoned there. The thing that hit me hardest was the pictures that American soldiers took when they first entered Dachau, photographs of these living skeletons who were sitting and staring at the camera. They didn't even have the energy to walk or to celebrate their liberation from hell.

As a photographer, I knew that seeing things was the point of the art form but that here was something no one ever wanted to see. And because the cameras had not turned away, I was seeing it now.

The experience was powerful and poignant. Here was a group of college students who knew each other and joked together and had camaraderie and laughed together, and now, looking at Dachau, were uncharacteristically quiet. What conversation was happening was subdued, almost reverent. What could we say to each other to elaborate on this horror before us?

I thought about how Dachau was just one of many death camps, and suddenly, the industrial murder machine that the Nazis had created, and that so many people had helped them to run, hit me. I felt it in my gut and in my heart and in my brain. The Third Reich had to rid the world of Jews and Slavs and unwashed people that were not Aryan. And they had done it here, where I was standing.

It also made me understand the story and the power of Zionism. Any people who are subjected to this kind of potential extermination would desire to have a place where they're in control of their own destiny and where people can't ever try to kill them all again. Zionism got its start in the late 19th and early 20th centuries. And was not because of the Holocaust. It was because of a displaced people, the wandering tribes of Israel, who wanted a place to call home because anti-Semitism worldwide was showing no signs of abating. The Jews were always a group of people that everybody blamed when they needed to blame someone for something that they didn't like in their society. So the idea behind Zionism was for the Jews to return to the land of their ancestors, from which they had been expelled nearly 2,000 years earlier by the Romans. They wanted a country where they were free to be their own people.

For me, as an emerging historian, seeing this reality in the light of Dachau made a powerful impression. And oddly, later, it would enable me to more fully appreciate the Palestinian story, of a people being expelled from their homeland. I would not come to grips with it fully until after a life event that nearly ended my life. Because I didn't have to critically look at it and put all these pieces together that I had been exposed to. But visiting Dachau was a significant time for me as a student of history, as a citizen of the world, and as a person on planet Earth.

Pepperdine was a Christian university, so I don't know if we had any Jewish students among us on that day. There were certainly Jewish students at Pepperdine. But afterward, no one wanted to talk about it because we didn't really know where to begin. We realized how privileged we were, what kind of safe and secure lives we had, and how we'd never had to deal with anything like what the people who died or survived in Dachau had to deal with.

We worried about inner-city troubles, but it wasn't like

the police and army were coming into troubled areas and scooping up all of the gangbangers and putting them into camps and then exterminating them. We lived under the rule of law, and we expected it to last. It was, of course, the very expectation that the victims of Nazi Germany had, that the law would protect them, until there was only one law, and it was, at its evil heart, illegal on every level you can imagine. German society crashed into this mad, dark abyss, and here I was, studying in the country in the society that had done this. I didn't hate the Germans around me for it, but this was 1974, and a lot of those who were around me had been here while the "Final Solution" rampaged through Germany and Europe. The main conclusion that I drew was that I could only be my own conscience when it came to judging history, and that perspective had to be expansive. The one thing I knew for sure was that I, and all of us, felt like we were lucky. Maybe we didn't understand before this visit to Dachau how deep our luck really was and just how big the stakes were in World War II.

As for the Germany I lived in now, the war was not completely over. The temperature had been turned down, and the Cold War made Germany into a divided country, with the Communist East Germany on one side and the more liberal Democratic West, where I was living, on the other. Which is not to say that everyone was happy in the West and sad in the East. I met West German political expression up close in my first semester when the price of a ride on Heidelberg's streetcars was going to rise from two pfennigs to three. The streetcars were the principal means of transportation for the city's students (the University of Heidelberg being foremost), and so there was a huge student demonstration where thousands of people came out to Old Town to protest the raising of the streetcar rates.

And I was there. I went down there with my camera because it was interesting to me. I set up in the no-man's-land between the police and the students, and I was taking pictures, trying to capture the tension and latent conflict in images. The German riot police were there in force, anticipating a riot over the raising of prices, but they weren't paying any attention to me.

Heidelberg – Demonstration 1975

Heidelberg – Demonstration 1975

And then suddenly, the police started to walk toward the students, and so, toward me, and I decided it was time to get moving. I went down a side street, and suddenly, there were kids running past me as I was taking pictures, and this tear gas canister came rolling down that small lane that we were in. I got pictures of the tear gas canisters exploding but luckily didn't get gassed myself. But, I saw the effects on some of the students who were blindly running past me with swollen eyes and tears streaming down their cheeks—it's not fun at all. And the speed with which it had gone from static to active on the part of the police was stunning and, again, a reminder of how quickly a society can change.

The police stayed in formation and didn't pursue the students any further. They stopped halfway down the lane and set up their cordon so people couldn't come back down the lane to go to the main square.

If you went to the main square, you would run into the police who were operating water cannons and who fired them at the protesters. After the protest, later that day, I went back into town and saw the white residue from the tear gas and the water everywhere from the water cannons. I also saw soaking wet protesters.

There were no prohibitions from Pepperdine or from our advisers at the Moore Haus about participating in protests, but Herr Doktor Luft explained the politics of what was going on in town. He said that that was not unusual for the student body to protest in such a way but that we should probably try and stay clear of all of that. We had two guys in our group who smoked weed and who were probably dealing drugs while they were in Heidelberg. They had long hair and beards and looked very early 1970s, and they went to the protest and were probably hanging out with the angry students. I could imagine them as anti-war protesters in the years before they came to Heidelberg. They were also two of the guys that were taking classes at Heidelberg University in German, so I'm confident they participated in the local university student political activities.

I only went to Heidelberg University once, despite my affection for *The Student Prince*. I ate lunch in the university cafeteria with a couple of Pepperdine students who were also very good German speakers. I went with them to the cafeteria, but I never interacted with anybody there. I just went to see what the campus was like. I let my eyes be my camera on that trip, taking in the images to allow them to develop in my brain later. The best way I can describe it as a California guy is to say that it was as condensed physically as Stanford with a mix of modern buildings and older structures, but even the modern buildings kept the culture of the older architecture alive. There were no Cubist rebels on that campus.

I was happy at the Moore Haus, and I was loving the social life of being a student in Heidelberg, prince or not. We would take our evening meal in a restaurant right at the gate to the castle, called the *Burgfreiheit*, which served beer and other drinks. Now, of course, we couldn't have beer, as dinner was sponsored by Pepperdine. So we had apple juice or water or Coke with dinner.

Heidelberg — Bergfrieheit restaurant 1974

Heidelberg – Herr and Frau Schmidt 1974

Then right after dinner, we would walk past the Moore Haus halfway down the hill to a little gymnasium that had a bar attached to it. The proprietor of this gymnasium was a middle-aged German gentleman by the name of Fritz, who stood about five foot two and had black hair and very pale skin, and we always referred to the bar as Fritz's. It was small and friendly, with tables around the edge of the room, which would have sat 25 people, in addition to the old timers table in the center, which sat another eight or so.

Heidelberg – Fritzes Pub 1974

Sometimes on Fridays, we'd eat at Fritz's, and we'd have spaghetti, which was the cheapest thing on the menu. When it was a special meal, we would get the schnitzel and perhaps a *kirschwasser* or schnapps as well. And Fritz did a great job of making it. But mainly, we went to Fritz's for a beer before bedtime. It was our social hour for those who were willing to have a beer, as the seriously religious Christian students didn't believe in drinking alcohol or dancing on campus or anything like that, and they were not part of the Fritz's group at all.

The real radical guys were off doing whatever they were doing, so this was the middle-of-the-road people that went down to Fritz's, both males and females. Now, for many of us, it was our first experience in really having beers, despite my dorm room bar at Pepperdine. Back home, I was drinking those sweet cocktails in Malibu that Jeff Powell and I created, but we weren't drinking beer. In fact, my limited experience with beer was not a happy one. I thought beer tasted awful.

However, I acquired my taste for beer in Germany, with the added bonus that it was cheaper than Coke. At the same time, I was like my parents in that when they went to different cities and different locations, they would collect something from each location. So, I started collecting and learning about beer steins. I had a crystal one that had a nice pewter top. And eventually, somewhere at the end of the first semester, I had my stein there, just as many of the locals did. I was such a regular at Fritz's that when I entered the bar after dinner at the *Burgfreiheit*, my stein would have just completed being filled as I walked in the door, and the locals already in the bar would rap on the tables as a greeting.

I was going to head back to California at the end of my first semester, but Stu and I wanted to give our dorm the spirit of the Christmas season. So we marched across the river to a forest and chopped down a fir tree, then carried it back to the house. Our route went straight past a police station, and we didn't know that chopping down trees was illegal in Germany. The police did not come after us, though Stu was worried that they might, as they had already interviewed him for "leaving the scene of an accident" when his drunk taxi driver had failed to make a tight corner and crashed the taxi into a wall. Stu did what any logical person would do and had walked the couple of blocks home.

So, with no problems from the German police for our tree theft, I headed back to California for the Christmas break. Many of the students traveled around Europe between the trimesters. Stu was introduced to a German family in Bremerhaven whose son had been in his hometown on a student exchange in high school. He met a German schoolteacher up there who introduced him to her first-grade class. They wanted to know about cowboys and Indians and if he knew John Wayne. So he met her class, and then, freed from his California attachment, he met her in bed that night. But that is his story for him to tell another time.

I was one of the very few who returned to the United States between semesters, and part of my reasoning for doing so was to see my parents, who had come back for Christmas as well. And they had a mission in mind, and it was to do with my mangled foot. We were going to go to Dr. Robert Kerlan's clinic in Inglewood, California, to have my foot looked at to see if there was anything that could be done for it.

Dr. Kerlan was the Los Angeles Dodgers' first team doctor after their move from Brooklyn to Los Angeles in 1958. He was an orthopedist, and he diagnosed Dodgers' Hall of

Fame pitcher Sandy Koufax with traumatic arthritis in his left elbow. His clinic partner, Dr. Frank Jobe, pioneered the elbow surgery for pitchers known as "Tommy John surgery," named after the pitcher it was first successfully performed on earlier that year, 1974.

Kerlan also became the team physician for other Los Angeles-based sports teams, including the Rams, Lakers, and Kings, and my father probably pulled some strings at Lockheed to get me in to see him. My parents had brought the X-rays of my foot that were taken in Beirut back to California, and Dr. Kerlan looked at them and then decided to take his own.

Doctor Kerlan looked up from his X-rays of my misshapen foot, then he looked into the eyes of my parents and then me, the 19-year-old in front of him, and he gave us two options.

He said, "One quarter of the bones of the human body are in the foot and ankle. There are more than 100 muscles, tendons, and ligaments along with countless nerve endings. This foot has seen a unique trauma that has broken and then seen all the middle bones of the foot knitted back effectively into one mass. We could re-break every bone and try to set them back into place as individual bones, but there is a high degree of risk that nerves would be severed and tendons unable to attach properly to restore normal working motions. There is a real risk of having a floppy foot with no control."

That was option number one. Option number two was to do nothing, for as Dr. Kerlan said, "Your foot works now, you will most probably walk with the use of a cane before you are 40, arthritis is a distinct probability later in life, but you will have use of the foot."

I didn't want to be in the hospital again, worrying about whether this risky operation had destroyed a foot that was currently working pretty well. So my parents and I decided to take option number two. I was not going to be a world-class athlete, and age 40 was a long way off. Who knew what medical help could be available to me by then? As it happened, I didn't need a cane, and my foot bothers me from time to time, but I get by.

So I enjoyed that Christmas in California with my parents and my sister, and I put the idea of foot surgery out of my head for good. I had also really enjoyed my first semester in Heidelberg and was looking forward to my second, as we were going to take a trip to a place that sparked my galloping sense of history. We were going to go behind the Iron Curtain to East Germany, and I couldn't wait to see this hidden part of history for myself. I knew how lucky I was, a knowledge that our trip to Dachau had made profound. Now I was going to see what was so great about life on the other side. And if people there were lucky, too.

10

GOING BEHIND THE BERLIN WALL

In January 1975, I headed back to Heidelberg to begin my second semester of my Year-in-Europe. I was feeling confident in myself and my place in the world, and I was looking forward to building on my growing love of travel and history. I felt at home in Europe, in the sense that I could get along and do what I needed to do, and that inspired me to be bolder.

So, when Herr Doktor Luft told us that our Big Trip of the semester was to Berlin, the part of the city in East Germany, everyone was excited. He pulled me into his office and said he had a small problem that perhaps I could help with. The size of the student body in Heidelberg had grown, and we would not all fit in a tour bus anymore. He said that he would need to rent a nine-passenger Volkswagen van to follow along to accommodate the overflow. And since I was about the only student who had international driving experience, would I be able to help out? I said of course I would help. Herr Doktor Luft had shown me his trust and confidence to ferry the other nine of us to East Germany, and I was very gratified that he felt he could ask. I was the only one of us who had an international driver's license and had actually driven internationally, given my experience in Beirut; I was therefore the guy tapped to drive myself and some intrepid comrades behind the Iron Curtain.

I was excited by the idea of going to East Germany. I was taking upper-level history classes in Heidelberg because that's what we were taught. Later, when I studied at the University of California Santa Cruz, I had all the credits, except for three, to get my history major, which is why I was a history major out of college. Before we went behind the Iron Curtain, our history class had been studying modern European history. And the Nazis and World War II had been a focus of our studies just prior to us going there. So we knew how East Germany had come to be. Now we were going to see what it really was.

So, we struck out from Heidelberg to make the 250-mile drive to the East German border, cruising along the Autobahn of West Germany at whatever speed we wanted to travel. I liked to drive fast, and the straight lines of the Autobahn were a driver's dream. There were places where you had to slow down, but for brief moments, I made that Volkswagen van go faster than it had ever gone. Of course, I had to follow the Pepperdine bus, a big blue vehicle we all, imaginatively, called The Big Blue Bus, so I could never go faster than it went, and it was going at, shall we say, a

German civilized speed—faster than one would travel on the interstate in the US! So in my mind, I was an Autobahn speed demon, but in reality, I was going fast for a Volkswagen van.

After stops in Cologne to see the cathedral and in Bonn to see the West German capital, we went through the checkpoint at Helmstedt–Marienborn, which was the largest and most important border crossing on the inner German border during the division of Germany. Due to its geographical location, this crossing allowed for the shortest land route between West Germany and West Berlin, which was our destination.

The border guards were straight out of East German central casting. Were they East Germans? Were they Russians in Eastern clothing? Nobody knows. But they were stern and surly. And they were young, probably our age or maybe a little older, most of them privates, but there were sergeants watching over all, grizzled war-veteran-looking guys whose faces told you they had seen trouble before. And didn't deal with it sentimentally.

The border guards were suspicious that everyone coming into the country had ill intentions, double checking everyone's passports for signs of forgery. One of the guys in my van had grown a mustache in Heidelberg but didn't have a mustache on his passport photo. We thought that the East German border guards were going to make him shave it off just to give them the option of deciding that his passport photo was a fake. Or maybe it was just an exercise of their power over "the West." The Voice of America, the state-owned international radio broadcaster of the United States, broadcast the values and virtues of the West into the Communist East every night. They eventually let him pass with his mustache intact.

There was another guy in my van, Larry, who had decided that the best way to enter the German Democratic Republic and make a great funny first impression was to wear a gorilla suit—and I thought I pushed the edge of the envelope at times! He was wearing it as we drove up to the border, but then, when he saw the starkness of the border crossing and the wire everywhere and the roughness of the demeanor of the border guards, common sense prevailed, so he took the head off his gorilla suit, as his passport photo certainly did not look like a gorilla. And surprisingly, the guards didn't react at all to the rest of his body being in a gorilla suit. It was probably just another sign of the decadent West to them. And to us, it was more high jinks than political statement, just to push those boundaries that we loved to push so much, to discover just where the edge of the envelope was.

We made it through the border and drove the 100 miles or so to West Berlin, and this road was not an Autobahn, by any stretch of the imagination. The roads in general were pocked and bumpy, and the Trabant car, East Germany's answer to the VW Beetle of West Germany, was small and squat and looked (and was) slow. We made it to West Berlin, where we stayed for two days, and we saw the Reichstag and the Brandenburg Gate, these places of history that loomed large in the world in which I lived, as not that long ago, they were symbols of German imperialism and Nazi tyranny. Modern European history came to life once again, allowing what I had learned in the textbooks to connect with what I was seeing and to mean something more visceral than a passage in a book. A picture may be worth a thousand words, but being there is far better.

I didn't drive the van into East Berlin, though. Instead, we all managed to fit into a different day tour bus and went into East Berlin on a sponsored tour. We drove through Checkpoint Charlie, through the Berlin Wall, and to the other side of the world.

East Berlin was the capital of East Germany until the fall of the Berlin Wall in 1989 and the reunification of the country in 1990. It was always supposed to be the socialist poster child, a city that symbolized the superiority of the Communist way of life. As a result, the Communist regime invested more into the reconstruction and design of its capital city after World War II than it did in much of the rest of East Germany. Their thinking was that their Berlin had to look better than West Berlin. We saw firsthand the difference between the propaganda images of the "reconstructed" East Berlin and reality. There were still bullet holes in many of the buildings and no glass-paneled skyscrapers like in the

West. They believed their own stories, at least until people who lived in Communist East Berlin started massively voting with their feet.

At the beginning of 1961, it was still possible to travel freely to West Berlin on the "U-Bahn" (subway) and "S-Bahn" (elevated) train systems. Although it was illegal to leave East Germany without permission, there were thousands of people—from students to upper-level managers—who fled to the West, seeing it as a gateway to freedom. This mass departure drained the East of the talent and muscle needed to rebuild after World War II.

According to US Army records, 10,000 East Germans fled to West Berlin in January, which rose to 34,000 leaving in July, and 36,000 more crossed over during the first half of August. Refugee statistics showed a flow of about 3,000 easterners escaping to the West each week in May. The Allies joked about how the East would stop this mass exodus. "What are they going to do? Build a fence?"

On Saturday night, August 12th, 1961, that's exactly what happened. The East Germans began building what became the Berlin Wall by putting up a fence to separate East and West Berlin. Buildings were demolished to make a no-man's-land. Barbed wire was strung overnight, dogs and soldiers began patrolling, and they started shooting those who tried to escape from East to West. Eventually, all of West Berlin would be cut off from East Germany in the name of Us versus Them: The Communist Soviet ideology of the

East against the Capitalist democracy of the West. Churchill's metaphorical Iron Curtain had become a physical reality.

Berlin Wall 1975

The subway lines were severed, the city was divided, and the border was sealed. The fence became an 11-foot concrete wall that by the 1980s, the decade in which it would finally come down, was loaded with motion detectors and infrared sensors backed up by minefields and anti-vehicle trenches. In the first half of August 1961, there were 36,800 registered East German refugees. For the month of December 1961, it was a total of 744. The wall had worked.

Or not, if you were on the East German side of it. The wall was built so quickly that families were divided overnight. And literally, so were houses. The Russians came through one night and bulldozed houses, some of which straddled the East and West border. So they would tear down the half of the house that was on the East German border. And eventually, the Western authorities had to pull down the other half because it was destroyed. The Russians just went through and leveled everything. And created this, this dead zone. And death was literal, too.

People, desperate to escape the tyranny of Communism, risked life or death to get across the wall. By the time it finally came down in 1989, at least 140 people were shot, died by accident, or committed suicide at the wall.

Berlin Wall memorial to those who died trying to cross 1975

To sustain the fiction that there "was nothing to see on the western side of the wall," West Berlin and West Germany were literally eliminated from the official maps that were created by the East German government. The people of East Berlin lived in a city that was dominated by this wall that would kill them, and if they openly spoke about it, they risked arrest by the Stasi, the State Security Service—*Staatssicherheitsdienst*, SSD.

It was a somber place to pass through as our tour bus advanced past Checkpoint Charlie. On the West Belin side were Americans, armed and ready for battle, and as we drove into East Germany, the guards, even though they wore East German uniforms, were Russian, and they were also heavily armed. It was a living symbol of the Cold War: Both sides armed to the teeth, standing face to face, and one side keeping their people imprisoned by an idea, more or less.

Berlin – Checkpoint Charlie 1975

We could still see bullet holes in the buildings in East Berlin, and there was still rubble on some of the streets left over from the ravages of a war that had ended almost three decades earlier. It was painfully obvious to us that the people walking on these shabby streets of East Berlin were not as well dressed as West Berliners. You could see the difference in the success of the competing economic systems in the eyes and clothes of the people, walking with no purpose in their strides under the gray skies of the East.

You could also see it in the buildings. There had been a housing shortage in the East, so the Communists built tower block housing estates made from large concrete panels that could not have been more depressing to look at. The existing building stock in central Berlin was left to fall apart and was not repaired at all.

East Berlin – Opera House 1975

The *Stadtschloss*, the former residence of kings and emperors, was torn down by Communist party leadership in 1953, despite the fact it could easily have been repaired after the war. Protests had been lodged from around the world to save it, so it probably caused the Communist regime no end of pleasure to tear it down. The State Council building was built on part of the site in 1964.

One of the funnier—in the sense that funny here is a very relative concept—came when the 1,200-foot-high TV Tower was built between 1965 and 1969 in the center of Berlin's *Alexanderplatz*. The planners of the tower had failed to realize that the sphere at the top of it would cast a shadow, and it was very much the kind of shadow that they didn't want. It looked like a giant cross and created massive embarrassment for the officially atheist East and prompted a lot of ridicule in the West. It seemed to be a comment on the blinkered vision of Communism itself.

We were very conscious of the police state that East Germany was, as there was this feeling of fear in the people you passed of not being caught doing or saying the "wrong" thing. So it didn't matter if we could see the Stasi agents lighting cigarettes in the shadows beneath the lamppost; we knew that our movements were monitored. We didn't have to see it. We just felt it.

We had an East German tour guide who boarded the bus at the East German side of Checkpoint Charlie, and who knew if he was really a Stasi agent or not, but he was very keen to show us the war memorial that they had built there to honor the Soviets. We all got out of the bus at the Russian memorial to see the grandeur of this thing, and we heard from our guide how this wonderful memorial was a gift from all the people who "saved" Germany from Western corruption after the Nazis.

The monument is in Treptower Park, a green space that borders the river Spree in the southeastern part of the city. It was built in the muscular socialist realist style favored by Stalin, one depicting an idealized reality: All the men are bigger, all the women sadder, and all the kids more innocent. It is the largest Soviet war memorial outside of those in the former USSR, and it is also a graveyard, being the tomb of about 7,000 soldiers of the Soviet Red Army who died here in World War II.

East Berlin – Treptower Park 1975

As you enter beneath a stone arch, you walk to a small statue of a grieving woman representing Motherland Russia. Then you continue along an avenue lined with weeping willows that leads up to two giant Soviet flags made of red granite and below which, two grieving stone soldiers stand guard.

Sixteen stone sarcophagi line a huge open area, with each sarcophagus representing a Soviet republic. When the monument was built in 1949, there were 16 republics, but one of them was dissolved in 1956, leaving only 15 republics until the end of the Soviet Union.

The sarcophagi are decorated with military reliefs and engraved with quotes from Stalin (in German on one side and Russian on the other) written in gold letters. At the center of the monument, there is a 40-foot-tall statue of a rugged Soviet soldier crushing a swastika with his boot. He carries a German child with its arms encircling his neck, and he holds a huge sword with his right hand, perhaps protecting the child from people like him.

After we dropped the guide on the East side of Checkpoint Charlie, the bus made one more stop on the western side of the wall. There were memorial wreaths set up on two posts, with another wreath in between them that was almost as wide as your arms could stretch. That's how big the wreath was as a memorial. We knew that these memorials were to someone who had died there or to a family who had died there. It was the cost of trying to find freedom. And it was a cost that families were willing to risk because life in East Germany was so oppressive to them.

Along the wall, there was a platform, five yards back from it on the western side, where you could climb up steps to the top and see over the wall. You could see the half-destroyed buildings on the desolate eastern side, 100 yards from this concrete wall. After seeing the contrast between the two halves of Berlin, we all could start to understand the drive to seek freedom by those living, or existing, in the East. It was another reminder of the freedoms and liberties we enjoyed that, at times, we take for granted.

On that same trip, we went to Prague, Czechoslovakia, a country that was also under Soviet rule but one which felt a little more relaxed. Maybe that was because the Czech people had had an uprising in the summer of 1968 against the repressive Soviet rule and had shown a measure of independence before the Soviet tanks rolled in to reestablish control. And that independence remained. You got the sense that the Czechs might be occupied by Communist brutes, but they were certainly not conquered.

The guide that we had on our tour bus in Prague wasn't so concerned that we knew the glories of the Soviet Union than that we knew some of the long history of Prague, such as the fact that the oldest glockenspiel in the world had been there since the 12th century. There was the magnificent medieval town clock, known as the "*Orloj*," which was mounted on the southern wall of Old Town Hall in the Old Town Square.

Prauge – the "Orloj" 1975

The clock is a fascinating mix of science and religion. There's the astronomical dial, which represents the position of the Sun and Moon in the sky, and then there are statues of various Catholic saints on either side of the clock. There's "The Walk of the Apostles," which moves figures of the 12 Apostles every hour, along with a figure of a skeleton that represents Death and who, of course, strikes the time.

The richness of Prague's life was not surprising since some kind of human habitation had been in existence on the banks of the Danube since the fifth century BCE, and by the time I visited Prague, the city featured some of the most beautiful buildings I had ever seen.

Central among them was Prague Castle, which began in the ninth century CE and was a seat of power for kings of Bohemia, Holy Roman emperors, and presidents of Czechoslovakia. The Bohemian crown jewels are kept within a hidden room inside it. It is the largest ancient castle in the world, occupying an area of more than 17 acres.

I loved the National Library, founded in 1777, a year after my home country kicked off on its adventure in democracy. The library is built in the Baroque style, featuring gilded balconies and colorful frescoes, but it was the books that got to me. Ever since I started reading for pleasure while in the hospital with my mangled foot, I had started thinking that books were utterly fascinating.

I admired the effort that went into the creation of books, from the work and knowledge of the writers who use their brains to fill the pages with thoughts, facts, ideas, hopes, and dreams, to the decoration on the cover, and then to see all these old leather-bound tomes from centuries earlier, preserved by people who valued them and stretching as far as the eye could see. I think I got more out of that library in terms of appreciating what its contents meant to civilization than anybody else on the tour. There was so much history preserved so well. I would have loved to have seen the Library of Alexandria in ancient Egypt or to wander in the Vatican Library. That needs to be on the bucket list.

We also saw a wonderful "monument" along the Danube River. There were these large steps, six of them, that were 100 yards long and 10 feet deep, and they led down to the Danube. We knew that we had a pretty good tour guide when she explained the monument to us. "Yes, those are Russian steps," she said. "This is a Russian contribution to Prague. There, the steps of Communism," and she paused. Then she said, "They lead to nowhere."

We knew at that moment that we didn't have any kind of state-sponsored tour guide, and we certainly knew it when we went to the Pilsner beer factory on that tour. We got to taste test Pilsner beer brewed right there in the city that gave the beer its name, and that was fun. That was a gesture made to us by Herr Doktor Luft because he knew his students at that point and knew that we would enjoy it, even though it wasn't a Pepperdine sponsored visit to the factory, and from my experience, at least, the world would have ended had they known about it. This was Herr Doktor Luft's middle-aged act of subversion, one that those of us who engaged in youthful high jinks certainly appreciated and which endeared him to us. Maybe it was the German heritage of Bismarck and Realpolitik to know the difference between practical and ideological. But it demonstrated to me that common sense sometimes beats it all.

I now knew enough about beer to also appreciate the difference between Pilsner and German beer. The bitterness was much higher in the Czech beer than it was in the German beer, more hops and a different yeast, I am told, but straight from the brewer's tap and into my glass, with its creamy head and spicy flavor, it tasted wonderful.

When I first arrived in Germany, I didn't know anything

about beer, but by the end of my second trimester—because most students only went for two trimesters—a group of us had a beer-drinking contest down at Fritz's in Heidelberg. It was the kind of contest where we were trying to see who could identify beers with the most accuracy. We had learned to appreciate the beer and not chug it, so this was a contest of taste—a beer drinker's contest and not a drinking contest. Five different beers were poured into identical glasses. And we had to identify all five beers—what kind of brew, where from, and so on. Like a wine tasting for beer. There was Pilsner Urquell, Paulaner, Marsen (Spaten), Beck's, and Henninger. There were all these different brands and different styles. And we had to identify which brand it was— and not only which brand but whether it was domestic or export. And we didn't know the brands that were being poured that night!

I am proud to say that I got all five beers right. I think one other guy got all five right, too. But everybody else only identified two or three. I had learned that you can have the same beer, export or domestic, and you can taste the difference between them.

There was one other tradition that was fun in Fritz's. He had a glass *stiefel*, which is the word for boot in German. The *stiefel* at Fritz's could hold two liters of any liquid, and the liquid favored most was beer. You would fill the boot with beer and put it in front of one person with the toe of the boot facing away, and they would start drinking while appropriately saluting the *stiefel*—the elbow tapping the table, the back of one hand tapping the side of the *stiefel*, and then their other hand grabbing the boot near the ankle to bring it up to their lips. When they took it away from their lips, they would pass it to the next person. And that person would start drinking. When that person finished, they would go to the next. The person who drank before the person who finished the *stiefel* got to buy the next *stiefel*, so you wanted to be the one to finish it if it was getting close.

We all got very good at learning how to breathe through our noses and continue to drink the beer. And, of course, you had to be careful when the beer got to the ankle of the boot. Because when it got to the ankle and the air went up to the toe, it would slosh forward into your face. If it went up your nose, you were done, and the next person would surely finish off the remainder.

We did that *stiefel* game a number of times, especially when my mom came to visit. My mom was fun at Fritz's, and we probably had 10 people around the table with Mary Todd. Those of us there that night had experience at that point—it took 11 of the two-liter *stiefels* to get around the table the first time. It had to be some type of record. My mother generously bought all the beers, and while it was a lot of *stiefels* to get through that night, it was a fun outing in Fritz's for everybody.

And, of course, since we were in Germany, we went to Oktoberfest and drank way too much beer there. Fortunately,

I think we rode all of the carnival-type rides before we had our four or fifth liter of beer! I still have a few beer steins in my home collection from those hazy days in October. Were you supposed to take the beer steins? I think the answer is no, you weren't. But I had an oversized coat, and I was so skinny that I could put two beer steins in each sleeve and walk around the place looking normal. So that was my little crime in the name of beer.

My second semester at Heidelberg came to an end, and so did my relationship with Sue. Most people came to Heidelberg for just two semesters, and I was staying for three, so we promised to reconnect back in California, but as I mentioned earlier, when I went to see her in Los Angeles, and confirmed she had moved on. I did have a sense of that as we said *Auf Wiedersehen* in Heidelberg – good bye - and not "*Tschuss*" that far more casual "see you later". After all, she was a senior and I was a sophomore, it only figured that her life journey would continue and not wait. And so it came to pass.

I was also saying goodbye to Pepperdine after my last trimester in Heidelberg. It would be my third trimester in the Year-in-Europe program, and I think to this day that I'm the only one who went for three trimesters. How I managed to pull that off, I'm really not sure. I think it got to the point where you had to sign up to go back to Pepperdine and sign up for your classes for the next trimester in Malibu, and that got me thinking.

When I was in my second trimester, in Heidelberg, I realized how expensive Pepperdine was relative to getting an education at the University of California colleges. My father was paying my tuition and that of my sister at Occidental as well, and it was costly. I had a job back in Malibu at the rec center, but that wasn't going to put me over the line. I realized that by using my grandmother's address in Los Angeles, I could be an in-state resident for the UC schools and pay the much lower state fees.

So I applied to a couple of UC schools, and on the form, it asked you to list which schools you wanted to go to. UC Santa Cruz was the toughest one to get into, so on a lark, I put it first. And I put UCLA second. I figured that I wouldn't get my first choice, but I might get my second. And I really wanted to get into UCLA. Instead, I was accepted to UCSC.

And so I knew I was going to transfer colleges in September, and it just made sense for me to stay at Pepperdine in Heidelberg for one more trimester. And they allowed me to stay because Herr Doktor Luft agreed—to paraphrase Sally Fields famous Oscar-winning line, "He liked me, he really liked me."

In my first modern European history class, he gave us the syllabus at the beginning of the class and told us these are the 12 topics you're going to have to write papers on during this semester. And each paper must be one and a half pages to two and a half pages long.

I got into the first one, which was on World War I. I

spent a lot of time in the library, and I outlined the military history of World War I and analyzed some of the political commentary and added it to the outline. By the time I had finished the outline and was ready to possibly write a paper, I had 21 pages of outline. So I went to Herr Doktor Luft, showed him the outline, and asked him what part of I should use for my paper. He read through it and said, "Just write this paper from this outline, and you're done with the class." He said, "Nobody has ever done that kind of research for any of the history papers in any of my classes." The title of that paper was "World War I Fought and Won?" While the class requirements had been fulfilled, I still wrote papers on the other topics as well. I enjoyed the discovery.

I continued to go to all the history classes because I was actually engaged by the world before me, and I could go to different places around Europe and do things and see things that I was studying. And Herr Doktor Luft saw that, and I think he was impressed.

One other time that also endeared me to the powers that be in Heidelberg also probably influenced my extension. I had $900's worth of traveler's checks, my hazard pay from my month in the Beirut hospital. And midway through the first semester, an emergency came up with one of the students, who had to go home. She had to get a ticket, and it was on a weekend, and there was no access to banks. So Herr Doctor Luft, on her behalf, came to me and asked if I could help out in any way, on a short-term basis. I freely said, "Yeah, let's go down to American Express, get the ticket, and I'll sign over my traveler's checks." It was just what had to be done. And so we got this girl back home. A week later, she sent me a check for reimbursement. So I was able to help out, and the minders in Heidelberg approved. And they remembered. I had not done it for any reasons of glory or to be the golden boy. It was all done behind the scenes. I saw someone who needed help whom I could help. And I realized that it could have been me, and so the message was clear: We're all in this together, and if we can't rely on each other in good times and in bad, then we're in trouble.

Heidelberg – Pepperdine Year-in-Europe class of 1974-1975

At the end of that second trimester, I made plans to go back to Beirut for one more visit with my parents. Things were heating up in the Middle East, as my love of history had me paying attention to geopolitics, though I really had no idea how bad it was going to get in Beirut. I didn't know how much longer my parents would be in the city, and I wanted to see them and it again, one last time. Little did I know that the civil war that would consume Lebanon for the next 15 years was about to kick off. And little did I know that "last time" were words that very nearly came true in a way I could not imagine.

11

BEIRUT PART TWO—MY BEST LIFE

I t was very dark that night in April 1975 in Beirut as I drove Karen home from the dinner that I had made for her as a farewell gesture before I headed back to Heidelberg for my third trimester in Pepperdine's Year-in-Europe program.

The three days of fighting that had rocked the city between the Palestinians and the Christian Phalangists had stopped, and we believed that we were safe. Or, at least safer. I was going to be careful driving Karen home and not draw any undue attention to us.

That idea went out the window as soon as we drove between the high walls of the Palestinian camp just down the block from my parents' apartment. The Austin's headlights lit up the road as I approached the halfway point of that block. I knew the gates into the camp were coming up, but the street was dark and deathly quiet. I figured we were OK, but Karen could probably feel my tension, as we were not chatting about our possible romantic future. The car was silent.

Suddenly, Palestinian guards came out of nowhere and were waving at me to stop. The problem was that I had already driven past them, and I saw them waving their hands in the air in the rearview mirror. We were now about 50 yards past the waving guards, and as I kept an eye on the mirror, I saw three more guys step out of the darkness and aim their Kalashnikov rifles at us. Then they opened fire.

The rearview mirror was shot away, rattling around and coming to rest in my lap, and the back window and windshield were blown away. I glanced to my right to check on Karen, and as I did, I moved my head slightly away to the left as bullets took away some of the headrest. Two of those bullets glanced off my forehead instead of going through the back of my skull.

I immediately put my foot down on the gas pedal and made that Austin go as fast as it could. We needed to get off that street right now. We were still in the line of fire, which was visible now, as tracer rounds were lighting up the dark as the gunmen aimed to kill Karen and me. The Austin America car is not known for its handling ability, and it came close to rolling over as I made a left turn at top speed, with the car on two wheels. The sounds of Kalashnikov rifles firing at us mixed with the tires screaming to keep connected to the road.

We could not crash here, or we'd be dead for sure, so I took my foot off the floorboard, downshifted, and the car righted itself, and we were now on all four tires again. I hit the gas hard to keep us moving down the street and away from the guys who were trying to kill us.

I was seeing red—literally. My eyes were clouding with the blood flowing from my forehead. I put a hand to my forehead and felt the warm current of blood coming from a hole in my head. I had been shot in the head. And with the blood flowing into my eyes, I didn't know how much time I had left.

All I knew was that we had to go even faster until we reached safety, before the bullet that hit my head caused me to bleed out and kill me. I heard Karen starting to breathe heavily, and with my adrenaline at full speed, I looked at her quickly through the crimson veil that dripped into my eyes and, seeing no obvious wounds on her face or body, I yelled at her, "You will be fine, but don't look at me!" I didn't want her to panic at the sight of my blood. I had to get us to American University Hospital to save our lives.

I took a hard right at the next corner onto El Rachidine Street, and we were on our way to the hospital with as much urgency as my bloody eyes and the Austin could manage. One of the main Lebanese army barracks was located on this street, a half mile up on the right. The army had stayed in their barracks during the fighting the prior week, giving literal permission for the sectarian violence to explode in the city. I wondered if now that the violence had stopped, they would be itching to make amends for their silence. Up ahead was an army roadblock, which consisted of wooden crowd-control barricades that weren't exactly gates of steel. The roadblock was manned by a couple of disinterested guards off to the side. It looked like they weren't going to do anything.

So, given the circumstances, I did what I had to do, and I ran the army roadblock and sent the wooden barricades flying. The soldiers did not leap up and start shooting at us. They could see that this little car with no windshield or rear window and which was pocked with bullet holes had already had a bad night and was not a threat to them. Or maybe they were under orders not to fire at anyone, as that could bounce back on the army and drag them into a war that I had a strong feeling was just beginning.

We sped past the barracks, and through my bloody eyes, I was looking for the left turn onto Omar Bin Abdul Aziz Road, which led to the hospital. Many of the streets in the Hamra district are one-way, but tonight, driving one-way the wrong way was the shortest route to the hospital. So I ignored the signs and raced down the shortest route, hoping that some huge army truck wouldn't suddenly start coming the other way. But the streets were empty. We were the only traffic in that part of the city at just after midnight.

I parked the car near the emergency entrance to the hospital, and with the engine off, Karen's heavy breathing was loud, making me think she was wounded or at the least in a state of panic. I did not know if she had been shot or what her condition was. I just knew that I needed to get her into the hospital right now. So racing around the car, I opened her door, scooped her into my arms, and carried her to the entrance.

I was skinny, to be sure, but adrenaline coursed through my veins and allowed me to carry her as if she was a baby. My head wound was continuing to bleed profusely, and the blood was now covering the front of Karen as well as we entered the triage area. We must have looked like we were on the edge of death as the admitting nurses ran to us and did a quick assessment. Seeing my blood all over the front of Karen, they took her first, assuming she had been shot in the torso.

Amazingly, she had not been shot. The only wound she had suffered as the bullets smashed into the car around us was from a small piece of shrapnel that hit her on the hip—and as it was right in the spot where a bikini would cover any scar, she could still model and go to the beach.

I had been the target of the shooters, and I had been shot. But as I had carried Karen in, and as I was still standing, the medical staff now turned their attention to me. They placed me on a gurney to assess my situation.

When I had turned to glance at Karen when the bullets were being fired at us, it may have saved my life. For in the act of turning to the right, it pulled my head slightly to the left at exactly the moment two bullets were headed toward my head. Those bullets grazed my forehead instead of slamming into the back of my head and killing me.

They had grazed my head deep enough to cause a concussion. And, as all head wounds are prone to doing, I had bled profusely. My bloody red eyes were a result of me seeing through a veil of blood as it ran down my face. The medical staff applied antiseptic cleaning to my wound and sewed it up with 10 stitches. Suddenly, the world returned to normal colors and to my normal blurred vision without my glasses.

The bullets had torn up the car, and flying pieces of metal from the bullet-riddled Austin, along with spent fragments of bullets, had embedded in my back. The medics removed 12 pieces of shrapnel from my back, but again, I had been lucky. None of them had penetrated deeply enough to cause any real damage to me.

While the medics were patching me up, Karen called her father, Andy, who in turn called my mother. Karen's family's apartment was very near the hospital, and Andy told my mother that I was fine and so was Karen, and he would take us to their apartment for the rest of the night. My mother wanted to speak to me, but Andy told her that wasn't possible at the moment. He impressed upon her that she should not try to travel across town as there was still shooting, and having one Todd shot for the night was enough.

This was the second time within a year that my parents had received a call that I was in the hospital, and having a mangled foot was bad enough. My father was still stuck out of town by the fighting, and my mother was not going to shy away from this crisis. Trying to keep a mother away from her son in a hospital after he has been shot is impossible. She was coming to see me.

My mother and her pregnant Australian friend, Lotus Brady, who lived in our building with her American husband, called an ambulance to come to take them to the hospital, which was a clever idea. The ambulance arrived, and my mother and Lotus and the maid and my dog, Sheko, went down to meet the driver. So did a group of gun-toting Palestinians. My mother grabbed the end of one of the guns and shouted, "What are you going to do, shoot me? You shot my son!" And Sheko, for good measure, growled fiercely at the gunmen.

They backed off, apparently astonished at being spoken to like this by an American woman and being growled at by our dog. They didn't like dogs.

Then the ambulance driver told my mother that since she wasn't ill, she and Lotus couldn't travel in the ambulance. Upon hearing this, Lotus unloaded on the ambulance driver with some choice Australian lingo, and he soon agreed that she and my mother could follow him to the hospital in Lotus's car if she tied a white dishtowel to her car's antenna.

Mary Todd saw her bloody and shot-up car in the hospital parking lot, and she and Lotus raced inside. The Lebanese receptionist greeted them with a cheery "That's our first American shot!" and Lotus let her have it with even more choice Australian. Then they raced on to find me.

241

I was very happy to see my brave mother as I lay on the gurney, and she was very happy to see me. As soon as she saw that I was OK, more or less, relief flooded her face. And mine, too, I suspect. We all went to Karen's family apartment for the rest of that night (it was after 2 a.m. by the time we got out of there), and as I had been concussed, the doctor had said I was to rest but not sleep. So I sat on the couch and drifted in and out of consciousness until daybreak. The ceasefire was still holding, so we all drove back to our apartment, where my mother left me with the maid. She was off to the airport to meet my father, who was finally able to make it back to Beirut now that there was a ceasefire.

When my mother met my father at the airport, he asked where I was, thinking that I had made it back to Germany as planned. She greeted him with the words, "Happy Birthday, Roger, your son has been shot!" There was a small, dramatic pause, and then, "But Blake is fine," she reassured him, as she also let him know that I had not yet departed for Germany. It must have been jarring, to say the least, to hear those two facts delivered together. His birthday gift was that his adventurous, accident-prone son had escaped again with what amounted to relatively minor injuries.

Lotus's husband had also managed to fly back into Beirut that day, so we all had dinner together at my parents' apartment. During dinner, the doorbell rang, and my father answered it. On the other side of the door was a more senior man from the Palestinian camp. He wanted to know if I was all right.

He told us that there was an underground training camp for Palestinian soldiers near the Mar Elias camp, but it wasn't his guys who had shot at us. It had been the trainee soldiers from the other camp who had used Karen and me as target practice. We also learned that the night before they shot at us, another group from the same camp had managed to stop another car traveling past their camp. They had killed the English guy driving it and had raped the woman with him and left her for dead. I realized that if I had stopped for these guys, the same thing could have happened to us. And it was possibly because of Karen that they wanted to stop the car in the first place.

The next night, my parents had a cocktail party, and someone made a toast to the bullet that had missed me. I did not join in, as I was still concussed, and as I had become a German beer guy, I wasn't interested in cocktails. It was my last night in Beirut, and I just hoped the ceasefire would hold so I could get on a plane and back to Germany.

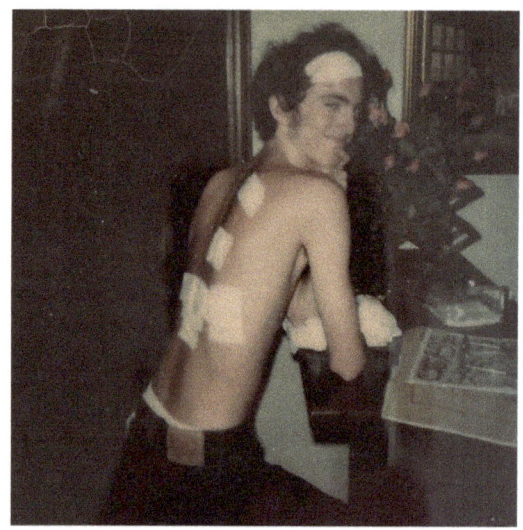

Beirut – bandages over wounds – April 18, 1975

Beirut – Roger, Mary, Blake and Sheko – April 18, 1975

Earlier that day, I had called Frau Ronsohoff because I was due back in Heidelberg to tell her that I was going to be late. I'd already been written up once in the bad books for not getting back on time when I went to London with Sue, and I had been warned that that would not be tolerated in the future. I already had a reputation for pushing the edge of the boundaries a little bit when it came to the rules, and that's what she was thinking now.

I could hear in the "what excuse are you going to give me this time?" tone of her voice that she was already suspicious that I was at my boundary-pushing again. I kept calm and told her I was still in Beirut and that I would be on a flight the next day if the planes were allowed to fly. But the reason that I couldn't get my originally planned flight was that I'd been shot. There was a pause on her end, and then she said, "Do what you have to do, and we'll see when you get here." She clearly didn't believe my story.

So I said goodbye to my parents, knowing as I did so that they would most likely have to get out of Beirut, too. They were already on it, as the three days of sectarian violence and my own collision with the Palestinian side made it abundantly clear that things were only going to get worse. In the end, my father was transferred to Lockheed's office in Paris. So long to the Paris of the Middle East, and hello to the real deal.

My flight made it out of Beirut without any missiles or gunmen trying to stop us, and I went back to the serenity of Heidelberg, where the worst I had seen was police hosing down protesting students with water cannons. But now I had to get past the gatekeeper at the Moore Haus.

Frau Ronsohoff greeted me upon my arrival and invited me into her apartment, which was not a common invitation for any student. That was her private space for her and her mother, and the dividing line was necessary for her sanity and ours.

As soon as I was inside the comfy and spacious apartment, she said to me, "I want to check and make sure your wound is OK." I think she thought I was wearing this bandage on my head as part of some elaborate ruse I had cooked up for being late. Little did she know there were also bandages all over my back from the shrapnel wounds, well hidden by my shirt.

So she pulled up the edge of the bandage and saw the stitches on my wound, and her eyes went wide, and then she nodded sympathetically as I told her what had happened. From that point on, I was the fair-haired child. "Oh, do you want some soup, Blake?" "Are you feeling OK, Blake?" She couldn't do enough for me, and I was more than fine with that. Even though it took getting shot in the head to make it happen.

A week later, I took the stitches out of my head myself with scissors and a mirror. And as I threw them away, it was time to tell myself that the bullets with my name on them had missed—and now it was time to really live. I wondered if our brush with death was enough of a bonding experience to tie Karen and me together in the way that I wanted, romantically. After all, as I got my last kiss from her in Beirut as I departed, she referred to me as her "knight in shining armor."

Beirut – Karen before our "night" – April 1975

I had been smitten by Karen, and she was in my thoughts often as I returned to class in Heidelberg. I held out hope that our budding romance could survive the ravages of distance that end so many relationships. But I wasn't going to rely on hope, so I wrote her a letter to remind her of her shining knight.

I came upon that place in the trees which I know so well and once again strode into the grassy clearing to relax my body and soul. Lying on my back, gazing through the trees to the formations of silver clouds which occasionally allowed the sun penetration to light the hues green, I was blinded by the warmth and lulled by the birds' sweet songs.

A rustling occurred somewhere in the bushes behind me, and the outline of a fair form moved to block my line of vision. The birds traversed the trees and found freedom in the open sky, but the shadows covered my face and then were not visible but in the mind's eye.

Her flowing hair created a tunnel through which I gazed into the bright, beautiful eyes of someone I thought was only in my dreams. Her hair softly touched my cheeks as her smile came closer. Ever so gently, with the sweetness of the springtime, she came closer to kiss my eyelids.

The rain smoothed over my face and ran down my cheeks; I opened my eyes, and she was gone. The bushes rustled behind me, and a rabbit emerged to scurry down the path, moist from the shower. As I strode through that same corridor of nature, I wondered if there could possibly have been something in the spring's rain which kissed me so sweetly—I wondered about you.

Inspriation Woods behind Moore Haus - Heidelberg 1975

Karen did not write back. At least, not as fast as I hoped, and not in any romantic way. She was at college in Maryland, and life was good. I was getting ghosted before the term was ever coined.

And so, life went on in Heidelberg, but Beirut came back one more time. The American ambassador to Lebanon at the time of my shooting was G. McMurtrie Godley. When we reported the shooting to the American Embassy, he requested that we keep it as quiet as possible. I was the first American civilian to be wounded in the current hostilities, and he really did not want an American making any headlines—or any fatal repercussions for Americans still on the ground in Lebanon.

We agreed to keep quiet about it. However, one of the students with me in Heidelberg was a journalism major, and she convinced me to give her an interview for an article. Taking into account the request by the ambassador, I was careful to withhold some of the details of that night, and so I gave as optimistic a portrayal as possible to the situation I had seen and which had nearly done me in. In fact, I was thinking quite a bit about that night and wondering about the perspective of the guys who tried to kill me. Why would they want to do that? And I knew a little bit about why, and it made me less angry at them. I could imagine being in their shoes. I just couldn't imagine shooting at someone, and maybe, given my own background and privileges in life, I could never fully do that.

From the May 1975 edition of *The Graphic*—Pepperdine University's student newspaper:

YIE student shot in Lebanon

by Sheryl Johansen

foreign correspondent

Despite having been shot and wounded while visiting his parents in Beirut, Lebanon, during spring break, Year-in-Europe (YIE) student Blake Todd said he would go back again if he had the opportunity.

Todd's family has been living in Lebanon for the past two and a half years. "My father works for Lockheed and is trying to sell passenger planes to the Arabs," he explained. "I've spent about eight or nine months in Lebanon."

"What happened to me was a scattered incident," said the junior political science major. Todd was fired at on April 17th with a Russian built sub-machine gun when he failed to stop at a Palestinian roadblock. He was released from the hospital the same night after shrapnel was removed from his back and he received 10 stitches in his forehead.

"It's a beautiful country," he continued, "and when you are there, you are literally swimming in history. But anyone planning a visit shouldn't go in April or October because then the weather is perfect for war."

The clash in which Todd was wounded began the week before he was shot. He said it involved a skirmish between two political factions—the Palestinians and the Phalangists. Although these groups are spread throughout the country, Todd said the fighting was centered in Beirut, where 150 people were killed and 300 wounded in five days of fighting.

He said that during the fighting, the American families living in his apartment building were confined to the premises. "We had parties all week," Todd said. "Every night we'd have a progressive dinner. We started our meals in one apartment, had another at the next, and so on."

When the curfew was lifted, he took out a girlfriend who lived in another part of town. When he was bringing her home around midnight, he didn't see a Palestinian roadblock and failed to stop.

This was when the soldiers opened fire.

Neither Todd nor his passenger was seriously wounded, but there was an estimated $1,000 of damage to the car.

Despite the incident, Todd likes the country very much. "The standard of living is better for the foreigner," he said. Having lived in California most of his life, except when his family lived in Hong Kong, Todd can see many differences between the Lebanese and American cultures.

"Family ties are strong for the Lebanese. The whole social structure is based on family. They think differently about bribes. They believe in favors in return for favors. When you go to Lebanon, you leave Western culture behind," he said.

And that last idea of mine became tragically true when Ambassador Godley was relieved of his post in March of 1976, and his replacement, Francis E. Meloy Jr., was assassinated while on his way to present his credentials to the new president of Lebanon. The civil war that started that week of my spring break in 1975 was only just beginning.

On my last night in Heidelberg, I went to Fritz's bar for a glass or two of beer, and in my halting German, I told him I was leaving for home the next day. He invited me to join the table at the center of the room, a hallowed space reserved for the regulars. It was, to understate it, a big deal.

They didn't offer that to just any students at all from Pepperdine. I was the only Pepperdine student to have my own stein at Fritz's, my cut crystal pewter-topped stein. And I was collecting steins at that point too, but it was almost like a bookshelf of steins behind the bar. All the locals who had their own steins had them lined up there, and now I was taking mine away. Back to America.

So I joined the table with these crusty old guys. I wasn't fluent in German by any stretch of the imagination, but I spoke halting German. And again, laughter and smiles can take you an awfully long way in conversation with people that speak a different language.

So I'm drinking a beer with them, and we're saluting each other with our beer steins. Maybe I was there at their table for 30 minutes. But it felt like a true honor. I felt like I was a real person from Heidelberg. I felt that I was in my commoner's bar, and I was the Student Prince. I was trying to be Everyman. And here I was, on the last night of my time in Heidelberg, at the center table with the regulars in Fritz's. *Ich Hab Mein Herz in Heidelberg Verloren*.

I think one of the guys did speak some English, so we were doing a little quick translating, and I found out that these guys were veterans of World War II. One of them was a U-boat captain. One of them had been a corporal in the Wehrmacht.

I didn't make the point, "You realize I'm an American, and we beat you?" That wasn't the attitude at all. It was interesting to see that wars created by the politicians, for whatever reason, from self-defense to world domination based on a crazy racial idea, are always served by the masses. And the masses really don't carry grudges, or know why they're fighting. Sometimes, they're just the sheep that are led to slaughter. War doesn't make sense for the average guy. That's the feeling I got from these guys, who had made me feel like the Student Prince on this night.

Karen, on the other hand, seemed to forget me. I had convinced myself that she was probably my first love, as I wanted to know her in a way that I had not felt with the other women whom I had dated. Sharing experiences with someone brings you closer, and we had shared experiences! She was at the University of Maryland and soon had her fair share of suitors that allowed her "knight in shining armor" to fade out of focus and then far and deep into the shadows.

When I graduated from the University of California at Santa Cruz with no job or prospects, I decided to try New York to see what I could scare up there. It was not because I loved the idea of New York but because Karen was there and had an apartment she said I could stay in while I was finding a job. And who knew what might happen if we were back in the same space again?

I spent more than a week going from business to business looking for a job but returned to California when it became obvious that any hope of rekindling our Beirut connection was not going to happen. It was a long and lonely drive back across the country in my VW Rabbit that had had its sound system stolen out of it while it was parked in New York City. Oh, how I could have used the sounds out of that beloved eight-track stereo as I drove almost non-stop back to the

Golden State.

As I grew older, my adrenaline rush of that evening in April 1975 in Beirut was replaced with questions of why me? And along with that question came another wave of the anger of an innocent who was targeted by violence in wartime. And then once I finally got beyond that anger, my curiosity and sense of history took hold as to the mindset of the people who shot at us that night.

The Palestinians had left their homeland and built the camps in Jordan and Beirut.

The children who were born in those camps were part of a displaced social group that was at the bottom of the social structure in Lebanon.

The Palestinians were engaged in what they believed was an existential struggle for their very survival.

The children of those camps were taught from the minute they were born that Israel was the enemy that would at any time send in their fighters to wipe the Palestinian camp from the face of the earth. And that no one would come to their aid on that day of their doom.

The kids were taught that other factions within Lebanese society see them as a threat and could attack them at any time.

So these children were trained to be alert for attacks upon them and to defend themselves from a very early age. It's what they have been taught; it is the only thing they know. It is their moral reality.

And the fears had been confirmed a year earlier with Israeli raids in Lebanon, which were revenge for what the Palestinian extremists had done to the Israelis at the Munich Olympics. The cycle spun on.

So when a threat on a dark moonless night comes down the street toward the gate of arguably one of the most important Palestinian camps, which is now near the training camp for militants and "freedom" fighters, their almost instinctive reaction is to shoot first and ask questions later.

While I may not believe as they do, while I may think that my moral compass and societal education are correct and theirs suffers from a lack of exposure to the rest of the world and more enlightened thinking, I can begin to understand their point of view and motivation.

I learned that in any situation, before I rush to judgment and take a firm stand, I should try to understand the other person's perspective, motivations, and needs. I know that there is indeed always another side to the coin.

If I could go back and change anything at all, I would not know where to start. So many things came together on that night in Beirut that were beyond my control. The raging forces of history, both personal and geopolitical, collided with Karen and me in that little car, and I was lucky to come out of the collision alive. And on my journey forward, I take with me gratitude for the life I was allowed to continue and which I try to lead as if it could, in fact, end at any minute. In that way, I can live my best life.

EPILOGUE

In writing this book, I wanted to tell you the story of how I was shot in Beirut once upon a time, as it was one of those life-changing events that also could have been life ending and yet was not. And so, because I had been given more time, as it were, I wanted to investigate what I had done before I was shot. In telling that story, I traveled back through my life to that point, and of course, to my life beyond it. In tracing my life leading up to that fateful night in Beirut, I came to realize that experiences in my life formed my values and beliefs. We all have experiences, perhaps not as harrowing as some in my life, but formative just the same. It is my hope that everyone can pause from time to time to take stock of their own life and how it was formed and to embrace their uniqueness and those special times in their life.

I wanted to tell you here, now, a little bit about how things turned out. I now live in Tallahassee, Florida, and am in the financial services business and have made a good life. I have a lovely daughter, a fine son, and recently a grandson. I am divorced, and hope still springs eternal where romance is concerned. In many respects, you might say I am still searching for that love with someone who will become my life muse.

My parents, both of whom you met in the book, are sadly gone but live on in our memories and hearts. My sister, Joyce, and I are very close even though we're on separate sides of the country, as she lives in California. She is still married to Reid, and they have two lovely kids, who are adults now with kids of their own.

Stu and I are still the best of friends, and we see each other whenever we can. He and I went on a trip together to Italy, Germany, and Switzerland a number of years ago. It was a reunion for Heidelberg and then an uncharted adventure. We were even able to have dinner in the cellar of the Heidelberg castle. We saw friends that we had gone to college with and friends we had made later.

And then we went off on a little driving tour, and we met up with the people that are friends of Stu's, and we drove down to Munich and met some exchange students Stu had hosted. We drove through the Swiss Alps, and we visited many castles, as I hope I made clear my fascination with castles as living testimonies to the past. We enjoyed one of the best five-hour lunches ever overlooking Lake Como. It was unhurried and a superb trip.

When I came back to the US after my studies in Heidelberg, I did not immediately resume college at Santa Cruz. I started not in September but in January, so I needed a job—and let me say, work is something I have always been willing to do. So, I managed to get a job with a construction company where my father knows one of the general contractors, Darryl Kahn. The last time I was anywhere near a construction site, I nearly lost my right foot. But I wasn't worried about that. I wanted to work.

Darryl's friendship with my parents got me what I will call a job audition. He had a small construction company and was taking a couple of dump truck loads of debris to the landfill. He had me drive the truck and operate the dump, which was something I had never done and, of course, was not licensed to do. But that wasn't the point. I didn't realize it at the time, but this dump truck adventure had been a test of how quickly I could take instruction.

I passed, for at the end of the day, Darryl said, "You now know how to operate a dump truck. If you are ever asked, you can say you can operate a dump truck." He then made a call to a site up in Fresno and arranged for me to get a job as a laborer from super-hot July in Fresno until January when I would go to UC Santa Cruz.

So I drove to Fresno and found a studio apartment in one of the sketchy areas of town a few blocks from the Greyhound station. It was my first apartment, and I had no furniture, so I grabbed a couple of two-by-eights to create a frame, and I put a waterbed mattress in the frame. I used boxes and milk crates to create the remaining furniture— tables, shelves, desk, and a table. During the days, I worked hard on that construction site. I have to admit there were partial flashbacks to Bahrain.

We were building a plant for a trucking company. It was

hot and out in the open. There wasn't any shade. I had to help build the forms and pretty much everything else as part of a team of three, with two Mexican American guys who were also laborers. The only saving grace was that there was no humidity!

One of the laborers owned 40 acres and had some grapes that he basically made into raisins. And when it was time to harvest in late September, he'd pick the grapes and put them on two pieces of paper right on the ground so that they would dry out and become raisins. He asked me if I'd like to earn a little extra money. I said sure.

I picked grapes for a weekend, and I learned just exactly how hard these laborers work. Using this razor-sharp knifelike instrument, I had to cut the grapes from the vine and put them down on the ground. I thought I was pretty fast, halfway down my row, but these laborers were finished with their row and on their second row by that time. You got paid by the number of rows that you finished, and many of them had families to support. Exhausted after this work, I appreciated what these undocumented immigrants were doing, as they certainly were not taking from society at all. They were giving back to it because they were providing the work that nobody else wanted to do. Hard, hot, demanding seasonal work that so many just turned their noses up at doing.

After my worldly travels and all the privilege that I had been exposed to, this was a profound lesson to me, and it made me realize that life's lessons were everywhere. You just have to be open to learning them.

When I landed at Santa Cruz as a junior, I realized that I loved to learn when I was interested in the subject. I had taken so many upper-level history classes at Heidelberg that when I arrived at Santa Cruz, I was ahead of the game and needed only three credits and a comprehensive exam to graduate with a major in history. So I took those classes that interested me, and I had fun.

In statistics class, I "proved" that the more peanuts that are sold, or consumed, in the stands at a baseball game, the better the winning record of the team. So my hypothesis was that you need to lower the price of your peanuts and sell more of them, or give them away, so that your team will do better. I proved it statistically to try to show that you can make numbers say whatever you want. That cause and effect are not always correlated. The professor was impressed.

Another class that I took saw UC Santa Cruz become a participant in the Model United Nations after I asked one of the professors to apply for it. We were assigned to Nigeria, but there were no classes or a professor who could provide the knowledge needed to prepare us to represent Nigeria. And so I volunteered to teach a class in Nigerian foreign policy. I knew nothing about Nigerian foreign policy, but I knew how to read, and now I loved reading. So I got some books on Nigerian foreign policy and read them, keeping a couple of chapters ahead of the class. In 1976, we went to the Model United Nations in San Diego, representing Nigeria. We were, in that year, in the middle of the oil embargo. OPEC was flexing its muscles, and Nigeria is an oil country—and a Black oil country. My team and I were co-sponsors of a resolution against South Africa. We won. I was having fun.

And this might surprise you, but at that time, I was also thinking of joining the Marines. I had met a recruiting instructor when I was living in Fresno, and he kept in touch. I wanted to be a Marine because I wanted to be a pilot, and this seemed like the best way forward. I knew that if I joined the Marines, they would take me through flight school, and I would become a pilot. But no, I wouldn't, said the recruiter. I have worn glasses for nearsightedness since I was a kid, and you can't be a Marine pilot if you can't see without glasses. But the recruiter got my hopes up when he told me that I could be a flight engineer. I was interested.

I traveled back to Fresno once or twice during that junior year to do some activities with the potential class of Marines recruits from that city. Just before I was about to go on my summer break from Santa Cruz, I was invited to go to Quantico for basic training as a Marine. Get basic done over the summer, and when I graduated, I would go directly to Officer Training School. I had to get on a bus in Santa Cruz to go up to Oakland to go back to Quantico. My alternative for that summer was to go visit my parents in Paris. I set my alarm clock for five o'clock in the morning to catch the bus to Oakland. Or I could wake at eight and take the bus to the airport to catch the plane to Paris. The alarm rang at five, and I woke up and said, "Nah, I'm going to go to Paris." Rolled over and got another couple of hours of sleep. I would not become a Marine. It was, just like the fact I could have been a track star, all about desire. I wanted to go see my parents in Paris more than I wanted to be a Marine flight engineer. It was another one of those decisions in life that you make and never know how life would have been different if you made the other choice. We choose our path forward and must embrace the choices we make.

I've had this conversation with people over the years about my life, and they say, "Wow, how interesting. I wish I could have done that." And then I will turn to them and say, "What was it like to have roots and have things that were predictable? And knowing what your community was and have lifelong friends? And go through school and experience life together? What's it like? I wished I could have done that."

Of course, I love the life I have had and do not mean to diminish any of it with that query. But in its asking, you can see the areas that I had to navigate going forward. Everybody's life is what it is. And you need to understand that it is special for you because it is yours alone. And acknowledge it and embrace it. The incidents in someone's life may not be in as exotic of locations, but that does not mean they are any less revealing to your character.

Throughout my business life, I have also had a certain number of restarts. Part of it is my industry. The firms kept merging or were bought out, or this or that, and there are a lot of new starts in my industry constantly. It's been a theme throughout my life.

You notice I say starts and not endings. I don't, as the saying goes, fly backward. I look back at my life and celebrate what I have done and where I have been and who I have known. But I live in the present, and I look forward. And as I do, I take with me many life lessons that came from those years leading up to my shooting in April 1975 and afterward.

I have, I hope, transmitted some of those life lessons in the telling of this story. They all pretty much come down to a couple of core ideas about how a person can learn to live with themselves in a healthy fashion, and so, in that journey, to live in a healthy fashion with others. By healthy, I mean accepting. Of yourself and others. And in that acceptance, to do some good for everyone.

I have had much that is good in my life. I have learned that we are lucky in life to have true friends, and if you can count them on the fingers of one hand, you're really lucky. When you find them, you need to put the effort in to keep them.

I have learned that testing the limits of society, of life, is no bad thing. So long as you don't hurt anyone, this limit testing might be the thing that makes us feel most alive. Sometimes challenging the status quo allows for breakthrough discoveries.

So, too, does history. You can learn not just about places and people of the past but how and why they lived. Travel does the same thing, as you broaden yourself and learn from others as you experience their different cultures. And in the end, recognize, as the photographs from the Webb telescope have so stunningly conveyed of late, that we here on planet Earth are a little blue dot in a vast universe. All of our differences and our distractions should vanish with that awareness. We should get along.

I recognize that life is complex and can't be boiled down to a series of slogans, and that's not my view of what I have learned. I have tried to take the essence of experience and distill it into a way of being and seeing myself in the world. And now that I have told you this story, you might ask me if there is anything I would do differently or not at all?

I would have to answer with a resounding "No." For if I changed anything, then I would not have this story to tell. It is mine, and in sharing it with you, I have made it yours a little bit as well. So let us take it forward on this amazing journey called life and see, together and with delight, what the next chapter will bring.

www.ingramcontent.com/pod-product-compliance
Lightning Source LLC
Chambersburg PA
CBHW051611120626
46551CB00014B/1752